SIEG HEIL!

SIEG HEIL!

War Letters of Tank Gunner Karl Fuchs, 1917-1941 · 1937–1941

Compiled, edited, and translated by

Horst Fuchs Richardson

Historical commentary by

Dennis E. Showalter

Archon Books
1987

First published 1987 as an Archon Book,
an imprint of The Shoe String Press, Inc.,
Hamden, Connecticut 06514

Printed in the United States of America

The paper used in this publication meets the minimum requirements of American
National Standard for Information Sciences—Permanence of Paper for Printed
Library Materials, ANSI Z39.48-1984. ∞

Library of Congress Cataloging-in-Publication Data

Fuchs, Karl, 1917–1941.
  Sieg Heil!: war letters of Tank Gunner Karl Fuchs, 1937–1941.

  Bibliography: p.
  1. Fuchs, Karl, 1917–1941—Correspondence.
2. World War, 1939–1945—Tank warfare. 3. World War,
1939–1945—Campaigns—Europe. 4. World War, 1939–1945—
Personal narratives, German. 5. Soldiers—Germany—
Correspondence. 6. Germany. Heer—Biography.
I. Richardson, Horst Fuchs, 1941–   . II. Showalter,
Dennis E. III. Title.
D793.F82213 1987   940.54′82′43   87–1327
ISBN 0-208-02141-8 (alk. paper)

Acknowledgments

To my mother for her willingness to relive the past, and for her personal commentary and invaluable counsel.

To my wife Helen for her patience and understanding, her critical comments, and her enthusiasm for this project.

To the secretaries in Armstrong Hall, especially to Lisa Dillon whose ability to read German script was a great asset and to Betty Welch whose computer skills proved to be invaluable. Many thanks.

Horst Fuchs Richardson
The Colorado College
Spring 1987

Contents

1.

Introduction by the Widow

The author of these letters, Karl Fuchs, was my beloved husband. I was married to him from 25 April 1940, until his early death in Russia in November of 1941. I became acquainted with him at the University of Würzburg where both of us were studying education. Karl's happy disposition, his sense of humor, his idealism, and his talent in music, especially in singing, made him a truly special person.

I assume it was his artistic nature and his enthusiasm for the new National Socialist Germany which first brought him to the Hitler Youth and then into the Nazi Party. In this he was greatly influenced by his father who was a restless romantic and somewhat dissatisfied with his life as a schoolteacher in a small village. Indeed, it was his father who dreamed of a better life as an officer. Karl was very much in favor of the National Labor Service and spent a mandatory half-year in a work camp in Bavaria. When he was drafted for military service, he volunteered for the tank corps because this unit seemed to be most important to him. His letters from the front speak of his deep love for the Fatherland and the strong belief in his Führer.

He was born in 1917 and as a youth grew up with the teachings of National Socialism. He was an impressionable young man and, like many of his contemporaries, was overwhelmed by the preaching of the party. He was killed on the field of battle during the height of Germany's war of expansion. Since he was such an idealist and a firm believer in the Third Reich, it would have been a bitter disappointment for him to have experienced the total collapse of Nazi Germany in 1945.

Helene Fuchs-Richardson

2.
Introduction by the Son

My father was a prolific writer of letters and postcards. As early as 1929 he sent his parents postcards from bicycle excursions he took through his native Germany. From a special secondary school for teacher candidates, located only fourteen kilometers from his village of Rosstal, he wrote about his academic progress, his love for music and athletic competition, and his interest in the social life at home. He was infatuated by the Olympic Games and listened to every radio broadcast about them. His pride about Germany's success in Berlin was evident. He became involved in the Hitler Youth movement, excelling in the athletic competitions which this movement provided for young people. Whenever it was possible, he came home to sing in the village choir or to play for the village soccer team.

His letters from the secondary school often mentioned his need for financial support from home. Also worrisome for my father at this time in his life were decisions about the future; university education, the National Labor Service, and the draft were immediate concerns. After he graduated from the secondary school, he joined the National Labor Service for a half-year. Then he completed his studies at the University of Würzburg and received his elementary school teaching certificate. After a brief internship as a village teacher, he joined the army on 1 October 1939. For the rest of his short life, he served his country as a member of the tank corps. He was killed in action near the town of Klin, just northeast of Moscow on 21 November 1941.

My father's letters from 1937 to 1941 provide a unique perspective of this important period from the point of view of a typical, young German man. He was truly devoted to the cause of Greater Germany and felt it was his sacred duty to engage in battle for this cause.

From the many thoughtful letters which my father wrote

during this period, I have selected these for publication. The first letters were written shortly after his induction into the National Labor Service; the last letters were sent just before his death in battle on the Eastern Front. I believe they accurately describe his hopes and dreams, his beliefs and plans, his reflections of occupied France and battle-torn Russia, his concern about securing a home for his young family, and the normal trials and tribulations of a soldier who is separated from his loved ones.

As a child I remember when my Grandmother Fuchs would read parts of the letters to me in order to show me how much my father had loved me. Unknown to me, my mother and Grandmother Fuchs saved the letters for their sentimental value. Many years passed before I realized that these letters had been saved and before my curiosity for them was aroused.

It was my father's intention to use these letters as the basis for a novel which he planned to write once the war was over. In translating and publishing the letters, I am not only sharing my father's thoughts, feelings, and impressions of these war years with the readers, but I have grown to know him, a man I never met. My hope is that he would have been pleased that his son had, at least partially, fulfilled for him his literary ambition—more than forty years after his death.

I would be very much amiss not to mention that these letters should also serve as a warning to future generations of young and vulnerable idealists. They, too, may be tempted and seduced by an attractive, yet evil, authority and pay for this brief adventure with their lives.

Horst Fuchs Richardson

3.
The Soldier's Assignments

Date	Location	Activity
April–July 1937	Schnaittach (near Nuremberg)	National Labor Service Unit 6/281
August–October 1937	Eltmann on the Main River	National Labor Service Unit 5/286
November 1937 to June 1938	Würzburg	University, Teacher Certification Program
July–September 1938	Mähring (near the Czech border)	National Harvest Service
October 1938	Rosstal (near Nuremberg)	At home
November 1938 to July 1939	Würzburg	University, Teacher Certification Program
August–September 1939	Zautendorf (village near Fürth)	Elementary schoolteacher
October–November 1939	Langwasser (near Nuremberg)	Joined army, boot camp
December 1939 to May 1940	Bamberg	Trained as a tank gunner, 2d Company, Tank Reserve Unit 35
June 1940	Erlangen	Tank gunner, 1st Company, Tank Reserve Unit 25
July 1940 to February 1941	Rochefort, St. Germain, Chartres (France)	Occupation Forces, military postal #06363
March–May 1941	Rhineland (near Bonn)	Officer candidate

The Soldier's Assignments (cont.)

Date	Location	Activity
June 1941	Lithuania, en route to Russia	Russian Offensive, tank commander
July–November 1941	Russian Front (Smolensk)	Tank commander, 25th Panzer Regiment
21 November 1941	Klin (near Moscow)	Killed in action

4.
Historical Comments
by Dennis E. Showalter

The question of exactly which Germans supported National Socialism before and after Hitler's seizure of power tends to be answered in collective terms. This in part reflects the academic community's growing commitment to the techniques of statistical analysis. Methodological commitment is often sharpened by ideological considerations. The moral rejection of Nazism throughout the civilized world encourages a corresponding concern for linking social groups of whom a researcher may disapprove as closely as possible with Hitler and his crematoria. Infrequent, and unpopular outside Germany, are conservative indictments of the masses as alienated, half-educated demanders of bread and circuses who wanted to "march—no matter where," and followed Hitler's drum in disregard of warnings from their betters that it would all end badly. The targets of choice are usually the middle classes, particularly the petty bourgeoisie, and the "Weimar establishment," that variously-defined mix of generals, industrialists, businessmen, and free professionals so often described as betraying a republic they despised.

It is hardly necessary to reject this collective approach to National Socialism to describe it as incomplete. Hitler's followers were more than statistics. Each had an individual story, an individual path to his or her own personal commitment. In 1938 the American sociologist Theodore Abel solicited the histories of rank-and-file Nazis by sponsoring a prize contest for the best essay describing the course and pattern of one's involvement in the movement. The resulting collection supports the contention that even hard-core Nazis were anything but faceless "mass men," human lemmings motivated by collective urges. Their decisions were the product of reasonable, if not always rational, calculations. Their commitments were based on perceptions of events that may have been distorted, but were nevertheless often carefully considered.

Equivalent evidence diminishes for the years after 1933. Partly this is a result of diffidence. Relatively few Germans have been willing to admit for public consumption that they found anything at all to approve of in National Socialism once it achieved power and began showing its true face. Personal memoirs from the later period fall into three general categories. The war story features a narrator too young or too naive to understand anything beyond the claims of comradeship and the dangers facing his homeland. Hitler is remote; the extermination camps are nonexistent. The warrior often fights not even for survival, but to sustain his honor in the face of disaster. The second category of memoir, the resistance story, introduces a different kind of hero. This author, either from the first or after the briefest of abstract flirtations, saw through the Nazi New Order and did everything possible to handicap its nefarious schemes. The results may have been minimal, involving little more than resigning positions or refusing promotions. The resister nevertheless expects full marks for effort. Finally comes the biographic *Bildungsroman*. Its protagonist begins as a fellow traveler, caught up in the parades and the promises, but somewhere along the line abandons illusion and hope alike. The conversion usually antedates Stalingrad and the bomber offensive just enough to absolve the narrator of the most obvious charges of abandoning a sinking ship.

The temptation to moralizing hindsight, even in honestly compiled personal material, reflects the ambivalence with which Germans viewed the Third Reich and its deeds. This ambivalence challenges, if it does not quite defy, the quantification process. In statistical terms a vote is a black-and-white, either-or statement. The motives behind that ballot, however, are likely to be significantly mixed. The heartfelt words of millions of Germans after 1945, "das haben wir nicht gewollt," were prefigured by a joke current in the Hitler years to the effect that toilet paper would in the future be stamped with swastikas "so the assholes can see what they voted for." The characteristic propaganda style of the Nazis, with its complex network of mutually exclusive promises, encouraged the tendency of interest groups to concentrate on their specific hopes and aspirations without much concern for larger issues. The flexibility, the protean character of the Third Reich, also encouraged hopes that problems of all kinds would eventually be solved—particularly given the air of no-nonsense energy projected by the Nazi Party at its lower levels.

Ambivalence involved more than abstraction. The ideologically based dynamism of National Socialism facilitated a certain populist obstructionism at the grass roots. Hitler's conviction that history's clock stood at five minutes to midnight, that only he could save Germany and the world from their imminent fate by crushing Jewry and acquiring the living space needed by his thousand-year Reich, led him to move in a hurry. National Socialism was initially content to control Germany's high ground, the individuals and institutions able directly to implement or hinder the achievement of the movement's ideologically based goals. In practice everything else tended to be left to itself unless something happened to attract attention. The elaborate Gestapo reports of public opinion never became the basis for a thought police. The concentration camp system was not a German Gulag. This did not make National Socialism indifferent to negative or fellow-traveling behavior. The movement simply had no time to deal with dissidents at the moment. After the Final Victory and the Final Solution, accounts would be suitably squared.

Ideology also operated to check domestic witch hunts. To a Nazi who took the party's doctrines seriously, the German people's only real internal enemy was the Jew. A German Aryan failing to see the light was more probably misguided than malevolent. Exposure to the *Volksgemeinschaft,* integration into it even on a compulsory level, would eventually generate not merely compliance, but enthusiastic acceptance. Over-assertive true believers at local levels were reprimanded more often than sustained when their efforts to remove crucifixes from elementary classrooms or their harassment of respected community leaders generated significant hostility.

The Nazis' long march through Germany's institutions, which began well before the seizure of power in 1933, was more than a pragmatic decision to turn toward the bourgeoisie and away from the workers. It recognized that National Socialism depended heavily for its continuing growth on the human touch. Adolf Hitler's emphasis on verbal and visual propaganda, as opposed to the written word, had its uses in making an initial impact. But the flexibility of the movement's ideology, the turgidity of many of its seminal texts, and the crudity of most of its newspapers and pamphlets combined to make sustaining these first impressions extremely difficult. On the other hand, particularly after 1930, an increasing number of Nazi notables at the grass-roots level were charming, persuasive, intelligent, and committed—a far cry from the hooligans who predominated among the *Alte Kämpfer,* and so remote from the party's public image among respectable Germans that their positive impact on their neighbors was correspondingly enhanced.

The *Gleichschaltung* that swept Germany after 1933, embracing neighborhood institutions from string quartettes to literary societies, was more than a move to consolidate Nazi power by stifling potential centers of resistance. It represented a positive approach as well: to integrate and convert by direct contact. Nazi true believers counted less on winning minds than on winning hearts and souls. Visceral, emotional invitations to join the marching columns counted more than arguments over points of doctrine or debates on the meaning of obscure passages in *Mein Kampf.* The ultimate appeal of Marxism is to the intellect. National Socialism appealed to the spirit. The radical Left promised a turnover. The Nazis promised a rebirth. A major appeal of National Socialism, one easily overlooked by critics, was that it took nothing away from its votaries. Instead it offered an extra dimension to their lives and identities—membership in the German folk community. In Hitler's ultimate New Order, the worker was to remain a worker, the professor a professor, the merchant a merchant. But none of those categories would be important. What counted was one's place in a biologically determined collective that put the deeds of every racially conscious German at the service of the whole.

To a Marxist or a Jeffersonian, National Socialism emerges as a confidence trick, a semantic game played on men and women not knowing any better. To millions of Germans in the 1930s, the new Germany was a land of promise beyond the wildest dreams of Republican or Imperial days. In this context the legacy of Karl

Fuchs is particularly valuable. It shows a good Nazi who was also a good man, an idealist whose death in 1941 left him knowing only the glory, not the bitterness. In reading his letters we see none of the hindsight, none of the questioning, none of the disillusion that infuses more complete first-person accounts. Though no such creature as the typical National Socialist existed, in both social origins and personality Karl Fuchs fleshes out the statistical, generalized profile of the people who supported, applauded, and sustained the Nazi state.

To understand Karl, it is necessary to comprehend his roots. His father was a small-town schoolteacher, a veteran of World War I, and a Nazi Party member since 1923. Hans Fuchs's early life reflected the changing face of Germany. He was born in 1892 in Nuremberg, a city emerging from centuries of political eclipse and economic decline to become one of the Reich's major industrial centers. Toymaking and pencilmaking, metal working and machine-tool construction, bicycle manufacturing and, after the turn of the century, auto manufacturing, gave Nuremberg a flexible economy and a reputation for openness to innovation. Not yet a *Grosstadt,* Nuremberg was more willing to live and let live than the average German hometown. It was a center of both middle-class liberalism and the strongest socialist movement in Bavaria. It remained a place where conflict was more likely to be resolved by compromise than confrontation—not least because no faction or stable combination of factions was able to dominate the rest for any period of time.

Hans Fuchs was part of that openness. He was born into an expanding *Mittelstand.* Germany's *Angestellten* tend to be characterized in parameters set by Hans Fallada: timid, resentful, anxious, petty bourgeoisie. Yet particularly in the 1890s, white-collar work offered vistas of opportunity as well. Germany was recovering from depression, moving into a global economy whose smooth functioning demanded more and more men with a mixture of business skills and cultural sophistication. Hans's father, beginning as a wage worker, had been able to become an independent businessman by opening a small restaurant. An expanding educational system provided the key for even better things for his children. Secondary education was not free, but particularly in the modern schools, the *Realgymnasien,* the costs could be met by judicious domestic economies. And in cosmopolitan Nuremberg a youth of modest circumstances would not suffer the kinds of discrimination he might face in a classical *Gymnasium,* drawing its students from the new rich and the old nobility.

Hans spent four years in the *Nürnberg Realgymnasium,* completing the sixth class in 1909. This achievement allowed him the privilege of serving only one year in the army, as opposed to two or three. In theory, Hans was also entitled to spend a seventh year in the *Realgymnasium,* then attend the university. In practice, a mixture of financial and social considerations made this impossible. Germany's universities might be open in principle to all academically qualified males, but even in Bavaria the sons of storekeepers or small businessmen were likely to find themselves excluded from the informal networks that were far more important than classes and seminars in determining future success. These problems might be outweighed by talent in specific cases. Hans, however, while a solid student, was not the kind of scholar whose teachers and relatives encouraged him to pursue an academic path. Nor was he interested in a purely business career as clerk, salesman, or bookkeeper. He saw an obvious alternative in becoming a teacher. Apart from factors of status and security, this profession appealed to the humane idealism of promoting culture even in attenuated forms, and the patriotic idealism of molding productive and fulfilled citizens of a modern nation. Hans began his training in 1909 and received his first appointment as a junior instructor in 1912. Two years later, at the outbreak of World War I, he was recalled to service in the Royal Bavarian Army.

Mobilized as a foot soldier, Hans volunteered for the air corps before experiencing the full horror of the trenches. Trained as an observer, he spent the rest of the war in the routine work of photographic reconnaissance, artillery spotting, and infantry contact, which might be less glamorous than the life of a fighter pilot, but was by no means less risky. His luck held. He remained unwounded and uninjured throughout the war. In September 1915, he married Frieda Wohlbold, daughter of a Nuremberg artisan. Bride and groom alike were twenty-three—a bit too young for a prudent marriage by peacetime middle-class standards, but war ripened relationships quickly. Their only son, Karl, was born on 18 March 1917.

Though Karl experienced his first months of life in a Germany marked by impending defeat, his father's patriotism and confidence remained unimpaired until the end. Hans Fuchs doffed his uniform with a sense of pride in his wartime accomplishments that remained with him the rest of his life. He was far more fortunate than many of his comrades. He had not only survived the war with mind and body intact; he had a job, and a good one. The Bavarian government assigned him to the *Volksschule* in Rosstal, a market town around sixteen kilometers southwest of Nuremberg.

Unlike his French counterpart, the German elementary teacher was not regarded as a bringer of enlightenment to priest-ridden peasants, or a representative of a central authority's challenge to provincialism and particularism. Nor was he viewed as a junior partner in a common process by the Ph.D.'s who staffed the secondary schools and universities. These men often regarded the graduates of teacher training schools as little more than jumped-up plowboys, Ichabod Cranes whose pretenses to *Bildung* defiled that to which they aspired. This lack of upward mobility might have been acceptable in a true *Klassenstaat,* a static society where God blessed the squire and his relations and kept everybody in their proper stations. But Imperial Germany opened just enough careers to talent, even on the lower levels, that those who failed to make their way tended even before 1914 to question the system that restricted their achievements. The influx of veterans after 1918 did nothing to reconcile German teachers with the wider society. Teaching offered two specific advantages to men fresh from the front. One was its promise of peace and quiet in an atmosphere of bucolic innocence—an attractive chimera to young men who had left their adolescence in the trenches. Another more practical aspect of teaching as a career was its use by the states of Germany both as a form of veterans' benefit and a means of freeing the educational structure as rapidly as possible from a generation of returning soldiers, who overcrowded facilities and academic routines.

Not a few of these men faced difficulty adjusting to the

practical frustrations of instructing as many as eighty children in a half dozen classes in their letters and numbers. In villages or small towns, the calm that seemed so attractive contrasted with life in uniform palled when translated into the reality of isolated, ingrown communities dominated by networks of families having no room for an outsider and his enthusiasms.

Hans Fuchs was a living challenge to the stereotype. His environment was a favorable one. Rosstal was a reasonably bustling market center. Its sons sought their living across Franconia, Bavaria, and the rest of Germany. Its parents appreciated education both as a means to an end and for its own sake. Rosstal was also Protestant; the census of 1925 listed only twenty-four Catholics among the town's 1,447 inhabitants, and not a single Jew. Like most of Franconia's Evangelical commmunities, it accorded its schoolmasters equal status with the pastor and the *Bürgermeister*. Hans in his turn worked as good teachers have always done, not for money but for pride of craft, and for what he himself called his honor. The contemporary academician complaining of classes twenty or thirty strong can only stand in awe of a teacher who regularly instructed forty or fifty students in eight or ten subjects without the help of classroom aides, specialized art and music teachers, and the whole spectrum of material resources taken for granted in today's elementary schools. Hans Fuchs became a leading member of Rosstal's *Turn- und Sportverein*. Taking gymnastics courses at his own expense, leading afterschool classes, giving private academic instruction to the slow or the gifted, doing building maintenance—it was a life calculated to bring all but the strongest and most idealistic to an early grave or to premature cynicism. Hans fell prey to neither. His former pupils spoke of him with admiration and regard as a teacher and a human being. School inspectors' reports praised his energy and dedication, his ability to inspire students to do their best even in the presence of strangers. Rosstal recognized his achievements and increasingly regarded him as one of the community's leading citizens, a man to turn to for advice and action.

This was significant because Hans Fuchs was a Nazi—not merely a sympathizer, but a registered party member, who joined so early that his membership seems to have been accepted as a given by his friends and family. Idealism has become significantly shopworn as a reason for explaining adherence to National Socialism. It must not, however, be dismissed out of hand. Hans spoke little of his motives. Among his intimates the most generally accepted explanation of his behavior is that his strong sense of nationalism and patriotism led him to identify with a party that proclaimed those values above all, while his deep commitment to the children he educated encouraged him to continue membership in a movement stressing the importance of Germany's coming generations. Particularly after the failure of the Beer Hall Putsch in 1923, National Socialism offered a refuge for idealists of the Right, just because it was unlikely to come to power and risk being soiled by compromise.

Hans's adherence to the movement may also have been influenced by his profession. National Socialism spread quickly and widely among the schoolteachers of northern Bavaria. The elaborate structure of Nazi ideology, with its complex formulae and polysyllabic vocabulary, is described as appealing to schoolmasters with intellectual pretensions. Studies of Bavaria's bureaucratic structure emphasize the tendency of elementary teachers to assert their status as professionals, to cling at least to the lower rungs of the *Beamtentum,* and to see educational reforms proposed by the Republic as threats to their status. Psychohistorians suggest the elementary classroom was a congenial refuge for authoritarian personalities, "bicycle riders" eager to fawn on superiors and bully those beneath them, projecting a whole spectrum of repressed hostilities onto Jews and Bolsheviks.

Realities were somewhat more prosaic. Hitler's right-hand man in Franconia was a schoolteacher. Julius Streicher's pathological anti-Semitism did not prevent him from being decent, even charming, on a human level. Especially in the early years, Streicher's vulgar platform persona differed sharply from his often gracious private behavior. In the 1920s, Nazi Party affiliation tended to spread among professional acquaintances and colleagues, and Hans seemed to have acquired a good deal of his politics by a process of osmosis.

Nor were Nazi attitudes and values entirely alien to Rosstal's political climate. Raw statistics can be misleading.* In the last national election before World War I, forty-one percent of the town's votes went to the Social Democratic candidate for the *Reichstag*. Between December 1924—the first postwar election for which Rosstal's statistics survive—and November 1932, the parties of the Left, Social Democrats and Communists, received a consistent thirty percent. These working-class votes were, however, overwhelmingly men and women who commuted each day to jobs in Nuremberg or Fürth. Their voting preferences represented an exception to the generalization that commuters residing in rural environments identified less with working-class values than with the bourgeois hopes of small landholders. This may reflect the fact that many of Rosstal's commuters were not displaced peasants, but urban out-migrants taking advantage of improved local transportation networks. Most were also cut off, by work schedules and attitudes, from the complex structure of relationships and exchanges that set Rosstal's tone. The local socialists were not so much regarded as a threat to the existing order as they were politically invisible.

The Nazis' success in Franconia has been accurately presented in terms of the economic and political uncertainties of the Great Depression working on a middle-class Protestant community possessing a significant heritage of protest politics from the days of the Empire. Franconia's Evangelicals historically viewed themselves as a bridge between Munich and Berlin. Critical of Bavarian particularism and Bavarian Catholicism, they tended to support liberal political parties. Forty-four percent of Rosstal's vote in 1912 was cast for the left-liberal Progressive People's Party. This political orientation, however, reflected identification with prewar German liberalism's nationalist and anticlerical heritage rather than any leanings toward democracy. While data for elections between 1919 and 1924 is unavailable, in the national election of December 1924, forty percent of the Rosstalers voted for the conservative German National People's Party. In 1928, the figure was thirty-two percent. During the Weimar period Rosstal's liberal parties, even including the right-of-center German People's Party, never mustered more than eighty-five votes among them. This voting profile also reflected the town's still-strong rural orientation. Parties appealing to peasant smallholders, the *Landvolk* and the Bavarian Farmers' and Middle Class League, were until 1930 relatively stronger in Rosstal than in surrounding communities with similar populations.

Rosstal's Nazi vote in the 1920s was not particularly high—forty-seven (7%) in 1924, thirty-nine (6%) in 1928. Relative to the rest of Germany, it was a solid base for the breakthrough election of September 1930, when the town's Nazi vote rose to 178, a quarter of the ballots cast. The movement's real breakthrough in Rosstal, however, came in the next eighteen months. In July 1932, two-thirds of the town's voters, 614 men and women, chose the Hitler list. With the left-wing parties holding steady, middle-class opposition to National Socialism had virtually disappeared in this one corner of Germany.

This drastic shift reflects three specific factors. A large part of the Nazis' success involved mobilizing non-voters, people previously alienated from the political process. In 1930, Rosstal cast 702 valid ballots. In 1932, 923 of the town's citizens voted. While there is no way to determine whether all of these people cast Nazi ballots, nothing in the town's voting patterns indicates that this new vote went anywhere else.

Slightly less obviously, Rosstal's middle-class voters did not turn immediately from their former parties to the National Socialists. The years between 1928 and 1932 were a time of general political reorientation in Germany. Parties changed names, programs, and structures with bewildering speed in an effort to retain old supporters and win new ones. Middle-class Protestant voters frequently cast at least one ballot for each one of these organizations before deciding they represented an ineffective response to Germany's multiple crises. In Rosstal, the real surprise victor in the September 1930 election might legitimately be described as the *Landvolk*. From a single mandate in 1928, this Christian-nationalist peasant organization increased its vote to 130. Another sixty-five Rosstalers voted for the *Christlichsozialer Volksdienst*, a moderate-conservative bourgeois organization whose goal was to create a Protestant equivalent of the Catholic Center Party. But neither could develop the staff, the speakers, the financial support, the publicity networks enabling them to compete in offering hope. Eighteen months later, both organizations had vanished from Rosstal, from Franconia, and from Germany.

Rosstal's movement into the Nazi camp finally reflects a significant bandwagon effect. An increasingly politicized everyday environment encouraged a kind of Brownian movement. As more and more citizens expressed themselves willing at least to give the "Hitler people" a try, more and more of their neighbors said "why not? Things can hardly get worse." After 1930 Germany's Protestant countryside faced a dearth of credible alternatives. Traditional party affiliations were difficult to sustain. Even if the party survived, its platform seemed irrelevant. Catholicism and Marxism were the major holdouts against Hitler's proposed New Order. Neither was likely to appeal to Rosstal's middle-class voters. It was correspondingly easy to shift support to an active, dynamic movement—particularly 'when, as in Rosstal, at least one of the town's leading citizens offered an example of Nazism at its best.

National Socialism was not a hypocritical movement. Nevertheless, before 1933 much of it remained abstract doctrine as opposed to exhibited behavior. Underlying partisan political activity in towns like Rosstal, moreover, was a general sense that people had to live together and get along no matter what election results might be. Hans Fuchs did not face major direct challenges to his political position, nor was he forced to observe directly such negative consequences as broken windows and broken heads. Nothing in his personal life or his professional career suggests that he was regarded as a fanatic drumbeater for Adolf Hitler. Certainly he did not seek personal rewards after 1933. His career took no sudden upward surge. He held no profitable party offices. Instead he is remembered as a man who remained a loyal friend, using his connections to help his fellow townsmen whenever possible.

Men like Hans, good neighbors, good citizens, good human beings, helped bring the Third Reich into existence. Boys like Karl sustained it. Peter Loewenberg has described the emergence in the 1920s of a Nazi youth cohort, reflecting a mix of generational conflict and childhood deprivation leading to a search for charismatic father figures. Karl Fuchs did not have to go that far afield. He was conditioned early to share his father's tastes for music and sports. From childhood he gained recognition in the local *Turn- und Sportverein.* From adolescence he made friends with his songs.

In commenting on an early draft of this introduction, his widow scorned this plain statement. It was, she said, something only an American would write, implying a *Stammtisch* vocalist able to carry the tunes of a few *Bierlieder.* Karl possessed a voice that under other circumstances might have led to a professional career, or at least to systematic training. In school, in the Labor Service, or in the army, the cry went up "Korri, give us a song." The song was at least as likely to be one of the classics as a folk tune or a party anthem. And when he sang, everyone admired him.

Karl Fuchs, in short, was the kind of young man often described today by the adjectives "natural" or "golden boy." He was neither saint nor prig. And the generational conflicts between father and son were hardly the heavy-handed psychodramas frequently described as characteristic of Weimar Germany. They were rather window-rattling, door-slamming arguments that, particularly as Karl grew older, could lead to days of strained relations and cold nods of the head in passing, but inevitably culminated in reconciliation. They did not encourage questioning of parental values, any more than the general climate of Rosstal fostered a spirit of political dissent.

From childhood Karl was a bit of a *Schwärmer.* His romantic, idealistic tendencies were encouraged by both parents. Anyone raised in the pragmatic, goal-oriented environment of the modern West can easily overlook the importance of this deliberate conditioning in shaping the mind-set of the German bourgeoisie. Far from considering extreme sensitivity the mark of a potential ne'er-do-well, mothers and fathers were prone to regard it as an indication of a lofty soul—particularly when it was combined, as in Karl's case, with physical fitness and high spirits. The formation of a detached, critical intelligence was of secondary importance. Objective observation of the New Germany's flaws and shortcomings were hardly to be expected from a sixteen-year-old in the peak of physical condition, possessing the chiseled good looks that were the Nazi ideal for males, who could play soccer and drink beer with the best of his age mates.

One of the major factors in National Socialism's successful governing of Germany after 1933 was the new regime's reluctance to change the routines of most of the ordinary social and fraternal activities that did so much to hold communities together. Instead, the Nazis simply added an official, political element to what was already going on. The faces in the groups remained essentially the same. Rather than abandoning an activity, participants found that it had a new dimension—one that could be extremely gratifying. Since the French and Industrial Revolutions, Atlantic societies have grappled with the problem of balancing individual achievement and group solidarity. "Do well" is one general admonition—but another is "Do not do too well, or no one will accept you." That Karl did not walk alone in his public life was due in no small measure to the Third Reich's insistence that the individual best served his community by fulfilling and developing his own potential. The effect of this principle at the higher echelons of Nazi Germany has been documented. On an everyday basis as well, it encouraged both cooperation and individual performance. The unusual cohesion of the *Wehrmacht* in combat owed much to the attitude, cultivated in Germany's youth, that the man who wore stripes or bars had earned them in direct competition with his fellows and was a correspondingly better man.

For Karl Fuchs, the Nazi order was a world of open doors. Hitler was a symbol, a name to put at the end of a letter. Jews were shadows. Like many country boys, Karl seems never even to have met one socially while growing up. His anti-Semitism, insofar as it can be said to exist, was abstract and passive. It was not a focused hostility or a developed antagonism. Instead, for Karl the 1936 Olympics prefigured the kinds of triumphs open to the sons of ordinary men in a Germany that shed overnight fifteen years of embarrassment at being German. His career plans remained undistinguished: to follow in his father's footsteps as an elementary teacher. But in Karl's mind this would be an ordinary life lived extraordinarily, in service to an ideal community that he saw as inclusive rather than exclusive, as affirmative instead of negative.

The first concrete test of Karl's principles came in the spring of 1937, when he became eligible for compulsory labor service.

The *Arbeitsdienst,* introduced in 1933, was not an ad hoc creation of National Socialism. Some form of national service had been widely advocated during the Weimar years, by Right and Left alike, as a surrogate for the now-forbidden conscription. National Service was also seen as a means of breaking down class barriers and as a way of providing work experience to youths rendered unemployable by the Great Depression—and not least as a means of performing some of the dirtier physical work that neither individual communities nor states had the will to do themselves or the money to have done. In 1931, the Republic established a voluntary program which included over a quarter-million members by the end of 1932. The Nazis continued and expanded the program, making it mandatory for students in 1933 and compulsory for all males in 1935.

Goebbels' propaganda machine stressed its role in building true socialism by putting everyone in the same uniform and giving them the same tasks, in service to *Volk* and Fatherland. In a Germany still generally uneasy about Hitler's foreign policy, whose males had historically—and sensibly—far preferred playing soldier to fighting in actual wars, the Labor Service became a symbol of rebirth even more acceptable than the new *Wehrmacht.* Spades were not rifles, even if they were used for close-order drill. Karl's father was an enthusiastic advocate of the institution. Karl himself looked forward to it with enthusiasm tempered by anxiety. How would he stack up against his fellows in the tests of hard physical work and a discipline known to be strict, if not brutal? It is in a Labor Service camp that the letters begin.

*Voting statistics are from Siegfried Munchenbach and Roland Schubert, "Das Wahlverhalten der Rosstaler Bürger in der Zeit der Weimarer Republik (1919–1923)," *Rosstaler Heimatblätter,* III (1981), 9–27.

5.
The Letters
Footnotes by Dennis E. Showalter

Schnaittach, National Labor Service Camp

6 April 1937

My dear Parents,

After two days here I finally have time to write to you. I have become somewhat accustomed to my new home and have turned into a real work-soldier dressed in gray. From 5 a.m. until 9, it seems that we do nothing but say "yes sir" and "no sir." Most of our superiors, however, are fairly nice fellows. At the moment we are undergoing ten days of preliminary training and next Tuesday we go, for the very first time, to our place of work. It doesn't look like we will have any time off before May 1st, but perhaps around Pentecost we will get five or six days of vacation. Naturally, I am looking forward to that! By the way, it is permitted to receive extra food from home! However, the food here is really quite good. In a couple of days you will receive my suitcase with my civilian clothes. I believe that this half-year of work service will pass quickly, especially since we have so much work to do here.

Well, it's time to turn in and we have to prepare our straw bedrolls. Preparing my bed in the evening is not so simple, but don't worry, I'll manage.

That's it for today from your national worker Karl Fuchs. I have to hit the sack! Heil Hitler!

Your loyal son, Karl

* * * * *

11 April 1937

My dear Parents,

Many thanks for your package. I have devoured much of its contents, since I get incredibly hungry while working. Naturally, you will be interested in what we do here during the day.

We have to get up at five o'clock every morning. After reveille we have fifteen minutes of morning calisthenics. In half-an-hour I have to be washed, dressed and have my area cleaned up. It is very difficult for me to make my strawbed in accordance with military regulations. If the bed is not made properly, the supervising officer simply throws the whole thing on the floor and you have to start all over again. Up to now this has happened to me just once.

After the cleanup of our barracks we have a hearty breakfast of ryebread and coffee. At 6:30 we start with drill. This normally lasts until 9. By the way, I was transferred from my original unit to a new platoon. I have been placed into the first row of this new platoon because dependable people are needed there. The new platoon leader, unlike my old one, loves to intimidate us with his tiring drills. But he can't break our spirit! The worst part of all this drill is standing at attention for long periods of time. Well, from 9–10 we have classroom instruction. After that comes second breakfast and a cigarette break. From 10:30–1:00 there is more drill in store for us. Then comes lunch. From 2–3 we are busy with general cleanup of the area, polishing our shoes, mending our gear, etc. From 3–4:30 we have physical education (mostly jogging through the forest), and the afternoon activities conclude with more classroom instruction and singing. Dinner is at 7. The bugle call for taps comes punctually at 9. Until then we are permitted to clean, mend, polish, etc. That was last week's schedule. Today is Sunday and for the first time we marched out of the camp in dress uniform. Under the supervision of the platoon leader we were able to spend some time at the local cafe. All of us work-soldiers enjoyed it immensely. The real work fortunately starts tomorrow. We are supposed to help build a road at the Schlossberg.

May 1st is our first leave. Perhaps I'll come home. You'll just have to be patient, especially Mother. She need not fear for the well-being of her "boy"; I'll return my old cheerful self. I could tell you a lot more about the camp but I'll do that another time. I do have a few requests; I need some spending money, postage stamps, socks and maybe some cigarettes. We don't get good cigarettes here and everybody smokes during the break.

I will close with my motto: "Keep your head up high, Karl, you old fox!"

Greetings to everyone at home. Heil Hitler!

Your loyal son, Karl

The above letter illustrates the paramilitary nature of the Labor Service's daily routines. In a country with Germany's history of compulsory military service, the drill and discipline was considered a rite of passage into adulthood at least as much as a preparation for combat. Karl hardly saw himself as cannon fodder.

Karl's request for money, stamps, socks, and cigarettes, a virtually universal constant for young men away from home, also reflects a significant connection between the Labor Service and the old Imperial Army. Conscription in peacetime was an alternate form of corvée, with physical service substituting for cash payment. It involved no obligation to provide a living wage in the sense of British and American professional forces, particularly since the conscripts were expected to have no dependents. The draftees' pay was essentially an honorarium, set so low that privates were expected to supplement it with food, money, and small personal items from home. The recipient of such largesse was expected to share with his less fortunate and less affluent comrades. In a well-run unit, his superiors made sure that this was done as a means of fostering character, comradeship, and cohesion.

*   *   *   *   *

14 June 1937

My dear Parents,

I am really not in the mood to write because I have been standing guard twice in the last seven days and I haven't gotten much sleep. So I am somewhat tired and, on top of that, it has been terribly humid for a couple of days. The humidity in our low, wooden barracks is hardly bearable. The hot weather has dampened everyone's spirit. Thirty of us, who are participating in the Nuremberg party rally, must practice two hours of dress-parade marching every day in the hot sun with shovels on our shoulders.

As you can imagine, we are sweating like pigs! The main thing, though, is that in six weeks we get to go to Nuremberg. After the party rally, it won't be long until our dismissal. . . .

In the rest of the letter Karl indicates a desire to come home for the weekend and longs for a plate of fresh asparagus from his mother's vegetable garden. The weekend at home, however, was not a pleasant one, as the following letter indicates.

*   *   *   *   *

24 June 1937

My dear Parents,

Since I didn't have much of a chance to talk with you on Sunday I would like to write a few words now about that "incident." I just don't understand how Mother can get so excited. I didn't "start things again with that girl," as Mother says. Sure, I admit I met with Rosl two weeks ago, but the only reason we met was to settle a rather silly quarrel and that is really all it was. Then Sunday, when I was home, I had to hear things like "Now you can see for yourself where you get your money for university study." I will attempt to clarify the situation with Rosl when I get home again in seven or eight weeks. On top of that, Mother said, "And what about Else? Have you forgotten about her?" I would like to remind you that you were the one who always said, "Come on, why don't you forget about that girl in Leipzig. That really isn't worth it." I never dreamt of ending that relationship and I don't intend to do so, especially not if Else doesn't say that she wants to. That's enough about that!

On August 4th I will come to Nuremberg to participate in the party rally. I won't be home again until then and I hope that these twelve weeks will pass by quickly.

Say hello to Fritz Bayn if you have a chance and tell him that he should visit me when he can. Be sure to tell him that he has to write ahead of time. Heil Hitler!

Your Karl

*   *   *   *   *

28 June 1937

My dear Parents,

On Sunday Rosl was here and we had a chance to talk. I was not surprised at all when she told me that Mother had discussed a number of things with Anna Weiss in a rather indiscreet fashion. I know that this entire matter must be public knowledge in Rosstal by now. I really don't know what I did wrong to make Mother so upset. I am of the opinion that as a 20-year-old man, I am old enough to take full responsibility for my actions, and I believe I have done nothing to be ashamed of. I also think that Father can understand me better and I am certain that he doesn't condemn me totally as well. At any rate, Rosl and I have settled things amiably. Rosl and I promised each other not to become involved again based on what has happened. Well, that's all. I don't know if Mother will believe me. At any rate, I don't want to say any more about it.

I would like to ask Mother to send me my soccer uniform, especially the black stockings, because on Thursday I have to play for the camp team. I don't need any clean laundry; I wash everything myself. Heil Hitler!

Your Karl

This letter and its predecessor indicate that Nazi teenagers did not spend all their time drilling and parading. They also suggest some of the enduring pressures of village and neighborhood life in Germany—a relatively closed environment which could make service in the *Arbeitsdienst* or the *Wehrmacht* a correspondingly liberating experience for the vast majority of young men who had no reasonable expectations of an adult life outside of the familiar milieu.

* * * * *

5 July 1937

My dear Parents,

I did forget one thing when I saw you last. We need to send my permanent address to the University of Würzburg. The Department of Education and Teacher Training also needs my current address and the date of my dismissal from the Work Service Camp. Would you be so kind and take care of this paper work for me? Also please ask them whether I will receive special admission papers or whether I will only need to go there for the examination. When you receive their answers, please let me know.

This Saturday evening there will be a farewell party here in Schnaittach at the Julius Streicher Municipal Pool since our *Reichsparteitag* platoon will not return here. But on Saturday I want to go home between noon and one o'clock because I am supposed to play for the Rosstal soccer team. Please tell either Fritz Weiss or Fritz Bayn that one of them should pick me up at 10 a.m. by the pool. I'm sure if they put their heads together they can find a motorcycle. Fritz Bayn should let me know whether someone can pick me up or not. I am depending on it. That's all for today.

Hearty greetings and Heil Hitler!

Your son, Karl

Since admission to any institution of higher education in Nazi Germany depended on satisfactory completion of a term in the Labor Service, Karl reminds his parents in this letter to comply with the stipulations of the bureaucracy.

Karl refers indirectly to the notorious *Gauleiter* of Franconia, Julius Streicher. Like many Nazi bigwigs, he was widely memorialized in public buildings and thoroughfares.

* * * * *

Eltmann on the Main, National Labor Service Camp

11 August 1937

My dear Parents,

I finally have time to drop you a brief note. I can only tell you that I now know what it means to be a soldier. My God, our drill instructors put us through our paces every day. I am not exaggerating when I say that we sweat liters. When I compare our present assignment here with the comfortable existence in Schnaittach, I must say that this is something completely different. Aside from daily drill and exercise, we also have to perform rather strenuous work. We are working together with private industry to complete a dredging project here at Eltmann. This project is really interesting. When completed, it will enable larger barges to move upstream.

Everyone of us has to complete a daily quota on the job. We have to shovel seven-and-a-half cubic meters of dirt in five and one-half hours; that's basically dirt that must be shoveled into little rolling carts. I tell you, this is quite a job. . . . Heil Hitler!

Your son, Karl

*   *   *   *   *

22 August 1937

My dear Parents,

All of us are very enthusiastic at the moment because most likely we will become the honor guard. Just think of it!! Our unit, the best platoon in the entire Reich! We would be up front whenever the Führer made an official proclamation; one hundred men from the *Reichswehr,* a hundred from the SS, and us—all directly behind the Führer. Besides that we would get excellent pay which we could certainly use during the party rally. On September 1st, we will arrive in Nuremberg and remain there for two weeks. Isn't that incredible! Now let me explain about the parade. Father will most likely sit in the reserved section of the Zeppelin-Feld. Only half of the original 40,000 labor service volunteers will march past the Führer. We will be the first platoon that marches by. Only the *Reichsführerschulen* are ahead of us. So when Detachment #5/286 marches by, I'll be in the sixth row on the left wing. Maybe you'll see me. On Saturday when I come home, I will explain it to you more precisely. I'll have to talk with you about something else anyway: a certain run-in I had with Fritz Wick at the town fair. I tell you, I'm going to get into a fight with that fellow before too long.

This afternoon my friend Ritsch and I will take the train to Bamberg and we'll go out on the town a bit. We want to look at the city and also go dancing.

I don't know yet if I'll be able to come Saturday, but Mother could send me one more package before the party rally. Until then, Heil Hitler!

Your son, Karl

Karl's marginally politicized high spirits reflect the fact that after the *Machtergreifung* the annual party rallies, held at Nuremberg since 1927, lost much of their militant aspect, at least to the rank-and-file participants. Whatever their theme, they became occasions to show off, meet and impress the opposite sex, and celebrate strenuously away from parents and supervisors.

In a letter written three weeks later Karl is looking forward to another rally with great anticipation:

. . . Just imagine, on the 22d of September all of us will travel to Munich in order to march past Duce Mussolini. We'll remain in Munich until the 27th or 28th of September and perhaps after that we will get a few days of furlough. At any rate, this will be a tremendous experience for all of us. It is supposed to be the largest display of military strength ever to take place in Germany.

*   *   *   *   *

University of Würzburg, Department of Teacher Training

1 November 1937

My dear Parents,

New student week is over and everything seems fine. Now we are all looking for apartments in Würzburg. After we were unable to find a place to live during the first day, we had to spend the night in an inn. After much searching we did find a room but only under the condition that we each deposit five *Reichsmark*. Lots of things have changed. It is no longer as easy as Mother thought, for instance, to pay the apartment rent at the end of the month. No renter wants to do that nowadays. Our apartment costs 20 Reichsmark a month for each of us. The apartment is nicely furnished and breakfast is included in the price of the apartment. Well, we have to buy the rolls ourselves because no landlord includes those. The other meals we eat at the university because it is cheapest there. One meal costs only 75 *Pfennig* there, but in the cafeteria you have to pay for each meal right away. Fortunately I received the money for food from Mother.

I know, of course, that it will be very difficult for you to give me the money for all these expenses but I guess there is no other way. Mother, be kind enough then and send me the 20 Reichsmark for the apartment and enough money for lunches and dinners for 23 days. Mother should also send my SA uniform, that is, the boots, brown pants and shirt. I also need the new pair of long pants to complete my uniform. I would also be most grateful if you would include a few glasses of homemade marmalade and a cake in the next package.

So that Mother doesn't think I am lying about the rent, I am including the receipt. Also included is a confirmation form for child support. Father should fill it out and send it back to the university and then he will receive 10 Reichsmark a month for child support. I guess it's better than nothing.

The opening ceremonies here were rather nice. The only bad thing is the fact that in order to join the student federation, we have to pay five Marks a month. Everyone is expected to join. Classes begin on Monday. Today is Saturday and Fritz and I took a little tour to his home in Waldhausen. To come home to Rosstal would have been too expensive.

I would like to ask Mother now to send my things and the money as soon as possible so that I will have all that by Wednesday. Please also include my two sports badges. Heil Hitler!

Your son, Karl

Student housing, endemically in short supply in Germany, grew even scarcer during the 1930s as the accelerated race of rearmament brought more and more workers into even a middle-sized cathedral city like Würzburg. The rapidly spiraling costs of rent are suggested by Karl's inclusion of the receipt to prove that he was not padding his expenses— another point of contact with the contemporary student world.

As a student and member of the SA *(Sturmabteilung)* it was important that Karl look presentable. Thus, Mother had to send the dress uniform. After the Blood Purge of 1934 the SA had lost the aura of activism and terror that had surrounded it during the *Kampfzeit*. It became one of the most innocuous of the Third Reich's mass organizations, membership in it being almost universal among males with any public function or public ambitions—a fact that often confused allied occupation authorities after 1945.

Joining the student union is another example of *Gleichschaltung* in practice. To remain outside of the National Socialist Students' Union involved making a decision to make oneself conspicuous, a position congenial to relatively few young adults entering an unfamiliar atmosphere.

*   *   *   *   *

13 January 1938

My dear Parents,

    . . . In March, during semester vacation, twelve fellow students (six men, six women) are going on a trip to Czechoslovakia. This is not a journey in the usual sense of the word, but it is meant to be more of a work trip for our Fatherland and our people. The requirements for the trip demanded that twelve students be selected who are brave and strong. I'm proud to say that I am among them. Don't worry. The trip won't cost us a penny and room and board is taken care of, too. (I could use a little spending money, though.) I do need a passport, however, and since I won't be twenty-one until March, I will need a confirmation from you, Father, acknowledging that I can apply for a passport. Please send this confirmation right away, and if you should have any information available on the Sudeten Germans, then send this material along as well. Naturally, I shall have to prepare myself for this trip. Heil Hitler!

Karl

    Karl's melodramatic description of his spring plans reflected Hitler's increasing pressure on the Czech government in the spring of 1938. The Sudetenland had long played a role in German *Volkstumspolitik*. Now these cultural pressures were becoming politicized. (See Ronald Smelser, *The Sudeten Problem, 1933–1938* (Middletown, Conn., 1975).)

*   *   *   *   *

18 May 1938

My dear Parents,

    In Würzburg things are going great at the moment, although we have much to do at the university. In seven weeks, about July 17, we have to report to the Czech border as harvest helpers. Prior to that, at Pentecost, our university soccer team will travel once more to Munich for two or three days. I am really looking forward to that.

    Now a few things just for Father. Last Saturday I witnessed my first student fencing duel. It took place at 6:00 a.m. You can imagine that we were all very anxious to watch. It was really fortunate that the fight only lasted for 20 seconds. Had it lasted any longer, it would have been a real massacre. After the signal was given to commence fighting, there was a short exchange. One of the students, while stepping backwards, suddenly thrust forward at the opponent's chest and at the same time the other student struck him in the extended arm. The attending physician immediately stopped the duel and indicated that the injured student was unable to continue. His arm had been slashed to the bone.

Otherwise, nothing new to report. Many greetings and Heil Hitler!

Your son, Karl

The traditional student *Mensur* was so surrounded by rituals and the participants were so systematically protected that wounds any more serious than those required to produce appropriate facial scars were rare. Encounters fought outside of the familiar framework with correspondingly higher risks of injury were not unknown before 1933. The new regime's emphasis on honor and toughness contributed to a significant increase in the number of such duels, until one notorious fatality resulted in the official banning of all student duels in September 1938.

* * * * *

17 June 1938

Dear Father,

Today I have a few questions: (1) Did you send some more money for me this week? I have not received it yet. (2) I've been informed that my honor award from the Hitler Youth* of the Nuremberg district has been reserved for me there. Would you be kind enough to request that they send it to you? This request has to come from the local party branch office. Please address your inquiry to Regiment Leader Konrad Uebler, Hitler Youth Regiment 321. I was initially registered in Schwabach. Please explain this to them and also tell them I am studying in Würzburg at the moment and that is why I would like to have my honor award sent to the local party office in Rosstal, since I am registered as a party member** there. Thanks for your help in this matter. (3) Doctor Heckel wrote to me regarding the medical certificate. Please tell him that I cannot obtain one at the moment since this week is

Student District Week and everything seems to be closed. Even if I could find a certificate, the medical insurance wouldn't be any cheaper and I would have to pay just as much as I am paying now as a member of the Student Association. Please tell him that. Thank you. That's all for today. Heil Hitler!

Your Karl

*Karl had been quite active in the Hitler Youth movement and had advanced to a leadership position.

**Member of the NSDAP, the Nazi Party.

* * * * *

Mähring (Harvest helper in the Oberpfalz)

19 July 1938

Dear Mother,

I'll write this letter quickly during my lunch break. Actually I wanted to write last night but I was too tired. Our excursion to the Silver Hut was wonderful! From there we had a marvelous view of all the German lands. Unfortunately my friend Ritsch was not along. As a matter of fact, he has not yet arrived here. No one knows why he isn't here.

On Sunday I arrived in Mähring. I was assigned to a very nice farmer and am well cared for. I have to work a lot, of course, but I enjoy the work and the farmer is satisfied with my perform-ance. I certainly am not afraid of physical labor. Yesterday we mowed hay, loaded it and brought it to the barn. The same thing was on tap for today. You know, their harvest is about fourteen days behind ours at home.

Mähring is right at the Czech border and many Sudeten Germans come over here. They are all poor fellows but they hope for a better life and believe that the Führer will save them from this Czech rabble. These six weeks here certainly will be no vacation. In spite of this, I want to work for our landlord at home when I return in order to earn some money.

Your son, Karl

Karl's dream of extending *Deutschtum* to the Sudetenland involved the prosaic reality of the Third Reich's annual mobilization of young people, especially students, as "voluntary" harvest help on Germany's small farms. It combined a gesture of Nazi support for the independent peasant with a statement of commitment to a *Volksgemeinschaft* in which everyone, no matter his social position, was expected to become directly acquainted with the soil of the Fatherland. Farmers frequently found the city boys more trouble than they were worth. Physical strength and goodwill did not always compensate for ignorance of the routines of a family farm, and as this and the next letter suggest, the teenaged harvest workers spent a fair amount of time sightseeing and celebrating.

*   *   *   *   *

21 August 1938

Dear Mother,

Many thanks for your postcard. Fortunately there are only a few days left and then we will be free to go. My God, am I glad that all of this is over! The last two weeks in particular were pretty hard on me. We had to work every day until 9:00 p.m. It seems I was soaked with sweat all day long.

Now tell me, what am I supposed to do with my old jacket? The elbows are torn and the jacket is quite dirty. If it is all right with you, I will present it to one of the farm hands here. He is from Sudeten Germany and I'm sure that he will be pleased to receive it. I think I'll also give him my brown shoes which I wore every day. By the way, I also need three Marks. I still have some money but I need the rest for a farewell party on Friday. Please send it right away, otherwise it won't get here in time. Give my best regards to all the people in the house. I'll be home soon.

Your Karl

Karl's offer to donate his jacket and shoes to the farm hand is another illustration of practical *Volksgemeinschaft*. The Sudetenland's economy, based on family farms, cottage industries, small factories, and regional tourism, had suffered heavily during the Depression. The region's *Gasthaus* wisdom tended to blame its problems on discrimination by a Czech-dominated central government—particularly when one was talking to *Reichsdeutsche*. There was just enough objective reality in the charges to keep them alive. (See most recently J. Brügel, *Czechoslovakia before Munich: The German Minority Problem and British Appeasement Policy* (Cambridge, 1973).)

*   *   *   *   *

University of Würzburg

9 November 1938

Dear Father,

. . . I simply can't understand why my failure to say goodbye upset you so much. A grown man must be able to restrain himself! In any case, you had no reason to say that I am exactly like my mother and that you want to throw both of us out of the house. I think you said that mainly because you were so upset. If this, however, is not the case, then I have to take the consequences. It's now all the same to me anyway. I will just quit my university studies and get a job somewhere as a laborer. But you've got to realize that I am no longer a boy and that I won't be treated this way any longer.

You, like Mother, will have to understand why I don't like it at home anymore. We have too many quarrels at home. I must say that Mother is to blame in many of them, but she is the one who has always taken care of us. You need to understand that she is nervous. You had no reason on Monday to scold her that way and did her a severe injustice. I don't know what Mother has done now. Has she really left home as she threatened? I know one thing for sure. Things can't go on like this any longer. Something else must be behind all of these blowups and anxieties. Do you think that it is the military? Well, it doesn't make any difference to me anymore. Heil Hitler!

Your Karl

P.S. Please send my papers for military service.

Back at the university, Karl refers to a family quarrel. Family tensions, accentuated by the difficulties and uncertainties of the times, led to quite a number of these family squabbles.

*   *   *   *   *

23 November 1938

My dear Parents,

Many thanks for the Saturday "shipment." I was very pleased and made good use of the contents.

What is your opinion of the current political situation? By

God, you should have been in Würzburg during this Jewish mess. I don't know if things were as hectic in Nuremberg, but we made a clean sweep here. I can tell you that the authorities didn't miss one of those pig Jews. You should have seen the insolent behavior of these Jews! Several times, for instance, some of these old Jewish hags spat right in front of young German girls! At any rate, it is significant that the whole world, with the exception of Old England, is turning against these scoundrels today. From now on, these Jewish gentlemen of the British press will think twice before firing on a German citizen abroad in order to hurt our entire nation. The people here were really upset.

This morning at breakfast we had salt instead of sugar in our coffee. Boy, that was some strange taste! Normally our maids take very good care of us but today they certainly made a mistake.

. . . Saturday evening our fellowship is having a mandatory dance out in Heidingsfeld and every member has to do his part so that it will be a success. I really need the money and clean clothes.

How are things at home? How did Rosstal do in the soccer game last Sunday? Greetings and Heil Hitler!

Your son, Karl

In October 1938 the Gestapo had rounded up and deported thousands of Jews living in Germany but possessing Polish citizenship. Refused entry by an anti-Semitic government, they were held in detention centers under the harshest conditions. Herschel Grynszpan, a seventeen-year-old student in Paris, learned that this had been the fate of his parents, who had been German residents since 1914. He responded by going to the German embassy and shooting Third Secretary Ernst vom Rath. This isolated incident was the excuse for a Nazi-instigated pogrom, the infamous *Kristallnacht* of 9 November. In Würzburg, students and party members took the lead in smashing windows, demolishing Jewish communal buildings that still survived, and manhandling women, adolescents, and old men.

Karl Fuchs, like most Germans, was hardly a rabid anti-Semite on a personal level. Days and weeks went by when he probably entertained no conscious thoughts at all about Jews. He was the product of two milieux where distaste for Jews in the abstract was likely to be strongly and frequently expressed: a Bavarian small town dominated by images of the Jew as Christ-killer and crooked cattle dealer, and a conservative and patriotic home where Jews were heavily blamed for the loss of World

War I. He had spent the previous five years not merely subjected to Nazi propaganda, but deeply involved in institutions and activities reflecting and embodying that propaganda. His adolescent patriotism had been encouraged to focus on the Jew as a national enemy. In this context, his enthusiasm for the *Kristallnacht* is understandable, though it was hardly universal in Bavaria. (See Ian Kershaw *Popular Opinion and Political Dissent in the Third Reich* (Oxford, 1983) 262ff.)

Nothing in the letter indicates that Karl participated directly in the pogrom and his widow insists that such behavior would have been completely out of character. The depth of his involvement in this aspect of the Nazi system is suggested by the ease with which his talk shifts to clean collars, soccer games, and salted coffee.

* * * * *

Bamberg National Labor Service Camp

10 January 1939

Dear Father,

Work has started again and the workload is unexpectedly severe. We are under quite a bit of pressure.* No matter what we do, we attract the officers' attention. They are really taking note of everything. Over the weekend we have to practice honor guard formation, i.e., no time off. Up to now, they haven't told us anything about our future and are leaving us in the dark. I guess we'll just have to wait. The first thing we have to do is to finish our officers' training course.

How are things with you, Father? Are you glad to be back in the service?** Let's hope that the next time we're at home together, family life will be more pleasant than usual. I enjoyed your Christmas letter immensely. The two of us do understand each other well.

We were notified today that we could volunteer for the Air Force until February 1st. What do you think?

When can you come and visit me? Saturday would be best for me. Write to me before you come.

I'm just sorry that I can't see my fiancée Mädi regularly.*** Do you ever see her or her parents? If at all possible, Mädi will be here Sunday. It surely would be wonderful if all of you could come together.

Well, it's bedtime. Let our battle cry continue to be—long live Germany.

Your loyal son, Karl

*Unlike military service, *Arbeitsdienst* could be interrupted for several recognized reasons, including participation in teacher training programs.

**Hans Fuchs was recalled to service as a captain in the rapidly expanding *Luftwaffe* at the end of 1938, and initially assigned to its signal service.

***Karl Fuchs first met Helene (Mädi) Schoeppe in Würzburg in 1937. Their acquaintance developed during the summer of 1938, when both worked in the same neighborhood as harvest help. Its progress was encouraged by Karl's imminent employment, his upcoming military service, and by what Mädi calls his "incorrigible" romanticism.

* * * * *

Rosstal

4 July 1939

Dear Mädi,

I've just spent some time improvising on the piano—Lehar, of course. Should I bring along the sheet music of his operetta "Land of Smiles" when I see you tomorrow? I already know the answer to this question and do want to make you happy. Are you looking forward to tomorrow?

While I am writing, I'm sitting in our garden. Blossoming nature fills my joyful surroundings. All is so peaceful and serene. Fragrant rose bushes and the lush green of the garden encircle me. This rural peace at home is something very special, my dear Mädi. I am much happier here than in the hustle and bustle of city life. I hope you understand what I mean. Of course, I cannot do without the cultural programs and entertainment opportunities of the city; however, these are only secondary when compared to a walk through nature's fields, meadows and forests, particularly when this walk is taken arm-in-arm with the one you love. I know that you agree with me. I hope that we can take another such outing soon.

In closing, let me quote the cherished words of a favorite

Richard Strauss song: "Wir gingen durch die stille Nacht."* Isn't this moving language? You see, Mädi, your Korri is an incurable romantic.

Love, Korri

*"We walked into the silence of the night," from "Nachtgang" (Opus 29, Song 3) by Richard Strauss.

This is the first of many letters to Mädi. Its language and style, which suffer badly in translation, demonstrate his *Schwärmerei*.

* * * * *

A Village School, during a brief teaching internship

Fall 1939

My dear Mädi,

I have just assumed my new teaching position. The winds of fate have certainly "blown" me into a "heavenly" village. I occupy a room in the schoolhouse, a room very similar to the one described so well in Goethe's *The Sorrows of Young Werther;* empty, cold walls, dirty windows without curtains, an old table without a tablecloth, a rickety old chair, an ancient washstand and a sleeping cot without any blankets.

My dear Mädi, I pray that you will never be assigned to such a God-forsaken teaching position! The village and the surrounding countryside are quite nice, and the people and children, at least the few I've become acquainted with, are likeable but that's about it! The widow of the deceased teacher, for instance, is said to be an alcoholic.

At school there exists a terribly chaotic situation and I'm very upset about it. There are no lesson plans anywhere and no record of what has been taught. I guess I'll just have to feel my way for a while. And just imagine, I have over eighty pupils! If you haven't been assigned a teaching position by next week, you must come and visit me. There is so much to talk about.

Now I have to work on my lesson plans. My God, I didn't think it would be so much work! Since I'm my own principal, I also have administrative duties and don't feel competent in this regard at all. And here I thought I would have time to work on my novel! That will have to wait.

Hope to see you soon.

Your Korri

The lot of a German elementary teacher in the villages had changed little since the previous century. Karl's description of his circumstances, with their tone of restrained desperation, parallels accounts in dozens of memoirs and novels. Erich Maria Remarque's *The Road Back* is likely to be the most accessible of these to English-speakers.

* * * * *

Langwasser Training Camp

October 1939

My dear Parents,

We've been at the Langwasser Training Camp since Wednesday at noon. For the past two days I wanted to call you but was unable to get through to Rosstal. On Monday, however, a sizeable group of us will parade in front of *Gauleiter* Julius Streicher and then march through the entire downtown area of Nuremberg. We expect to have a day off on Saturday or Sunday and I will call you then. Hopefully we will be able to meet. I have met a lot of my old friends here and everything is fine. Heil Hitler!

Karl

Karl's stint as an elementary teacher was brief. With the other twenty-year-olds of his *Jahrgang,* he was conscripted into the *Wehrmacht* in October. Fall was the traditional season for inducting Europe's draftees, after the harvest was completed. Germany had invaded Poland on 1 September.

* * * * *

Fall 1939

Dear Father,

A week has gone by and we're now settled in at the military installation. The entire compound is superb!* We have had our psychological examinations** and, based upon these tests, I was assigned as a tank gunner. Now, of course, we have to learn and train until we perfect all of our skills. Infantry training is almost behind us and in eight weeks we have to be fit for combat. You, as an old soldier, know best what this means. The intensity of training is tremendous and there is no rest for anyone. All of us are eager to make progress and no one complains, least of all your son. You won't ever have to be ashamed of me; you can depend on me.

Several days ago I had to report to the captain of our company and speak to him about my plans for officer training. Today for the first time we had to practice pistol shooting—five shots and five bull's-eyes for me! Next week we have training in shooting with rifles and machine guns. The recruits are looking forward to this training. All of us tank gunners need to be crack shots.

Next week we'll be able to climb into our tanks for the first time. Operating the vehicle will have to become second nature to us. Tanks are really awesome!

For the time being we will have no furlough, at least not until New Year's. Christmastime will be spent in our barracks. I hope that all is well at home. Please write to me if you are able to come and visit. One more request; please take care of Mädi so that she doesn't feel so alone.*** That's all for today. Sieg Heil and on to old England!

Your loyal son, Karl

*Karl's enthusiasm for the military base was more than adolescent patriotism. Hitler's *Wehrmacht* benefited from dozens of new barracks complexes, built to replace Imperial structures demolished or converted to other purposes under a Weimar Republic whose army was restricted to 100,000 men. Some of them are still in use, primarily to house British and American troops. While these facilities seem primitive to their present occupants, in the 1930s they were considered state of the art, often superior to anything the recruits had at home.

**What Karl calls "psychological examinations" were far less formal in the *Wehrmacht* than their contemporary British or American equivalents. They involved a series of conversations designed to enable a general assessment of the recruit's character and interests. Men were also assigned by the training officers to various special units during the first weeks of service.

***At this time Mädi is teaching elementary school in the village of Sack near Fürth. Since Hans Fuchs was an experienced teacher now stationed in the *Luftwaffe* at Fürth, Karl's request was a natural one. Mädi, by the way, got along famously with her future father-in-law. Mädi and Karl were formally engaged in January 1940.

* * * * *

Bamberg Army Base

8 December 1939

Dear Mother,

Many thanks for your letter and the parcel. I liked both very much. But Mother, I must tell you that I really don't need food parcels here. We have so much to eat that additional food is really unnecessary. When a package arrives, of course, I share the contents with all my comrades as is the custom. That is not to say that you shouldn't send something every now and then but just don't get into a weekly habit.

A week has gone by and all of us seem to already be real-live soldiers and we do our duty enthusiastically. Our camp and the barracks are really nice and we have no complaints.

You wrote in your letter that you want to come and see me at Christmastime. Look, there is really no sense in that because you won't be permitted to enter the camp and I won't be able to get out. So why don't we just wait until New Year's because that's when we are scheduled to receive some furlough.

Our entire unit will celebrate Christmas together. Of course, we intend to buy a small Christmas tree. This will be my first Christmas Eve in the military. Who knows how many others will follow! I guess it doesn't matter. Our duty is to defend our Fatherland. I am just as certain that we will fulfill our duty as I am about me becoming a good soldier.

Well, good night. I have to report to my room now. It's time for lights-out. Greetings.

Your son, Karl

During Karl's Labor Service days he welcomed packages from home (see letter of 11 April 1937). His changed attitude suggests a mixture of increased maturity and dislike of the risk of being singled out as a mama's boy by more calloused or less fortunate recruits. It also reflects the high level of *Wehrmacht* rations at this stage of World War II.

* * * * *

13 December 1939

Dear Mother,

A cold wind is whistling outside our barracks today. Believe me, it's no cakewalk to stand guard in this kind of weather from 7:00 until noon with full military uniform, steel helmet on your head, rifle ready and your cartridge belt and bayonet slung around your shoulder and hip.

Today is Wednesday and we were sworn in as soldiers. This was obviously a memorable experience for us, especially for me. While all the other comrades marched to the square where we were to be sworn in, another soldier and I were selected for a special task; we drove with a small tank to that square and looked out from the turret with our eyes bright and hands saluting the officers. This was a tremendous honor for me and I will cherish it forever. That's all for today. Heil Hitler!

Your son, Karl

German recruits were formally sworn into service only after completing basic training. The oath was often taken in the presence of a flag or weapon symbolizing the new soldier's branch of service; in Karl's case, a tank. His selection to drive the vehicle (an obsolete Mark I) onto the parade ground reflected his success in completing the basic training program—a success manifested more concretely in his selection as an officer candidate.

* * * * *

Christmas 1939

Dear Father,

This Christmas is a rather unusual holiday for both of us; we are away from home and are celebrating Christmas simply at our respective bases. If all goes well, we will be home next year, celebrating Christmas together once more.

The pupils from my former elementary school wrote to me,

wishing me a Merry Christmas. I was very pleased. I grew fond of them in that short period of teaching. Did I ever tell you that I had a major argument with the pastor of the village?* I'll tell you more about this when I see you.

What is uppermost in our minds this Christmas is adherence to duty to our beloved Führer and to our Fatherland to our last dying breath. May this sense of duty and a quiet handshake between us be our mutual Christmas greeting. Heil Hitler!

Your loyal son, Karl

*Such arguments were a universal constant in rural Germany. The career of Julius Streicher, who began life as a village schoolmaster, was significantly influenced by a series of acrimonious debates with supervising clerics. Under the Third Reich, local party leaders often became involved in complicated parish-pump conflicts involving teachers and pastors, "new men" and traditional community elites. (Cf. Elmer R. Peterson, *The Limits of Hitler's Power* (Princeton, 1966), 295ff.)

*   *   *   *   *

December 1939

Dear Father,

You called the base yesterday and apparently my superiors gave you a negative reply. I, in turn, have gone to all the possible offices and to all my superiors, trying to reverse their decision. They are very kind to me, yet the fact remains that they cannot let me go home by train, according to the decisions made by the Federal Railway. I have explained to the First Sergeant that you, Father, would pick me up by car. They would agree to this under one condition: you must send them a written explanation, stating that you are going to pick me up and bring me back. Then I would be allowed to go on this special furlough.* Now my question is if you can do all this? I really have a great deal to talk to you about and I would also like to be with my fiancée and with Mother on New Year's. It's up to you whether or not I can spend New Year's with all of you and at the same time celebrate my engagement. I could make the return trip on a bicycle. The tricky thing, of course, is that no one around here knows whether or not we'll be at the front in a couple of weeks.

After Christmas I'm supposed to join the officer candidates.** What do you have to say about that? Should I go to officers' training school? I've spoken with my platoon leader about this. He really likes me, especially since I'm one of his best marksmen.

Well, it's time to hit the sack. I really hope you can pick me up.

Your loyal son, Karl

*Red tape was at least as familiar to the *Landser* as to the G.I. Karl's holiday plans floundered because of wartime restrictions on train travel during the holidays. How his father proposed to get enough rationed gasoline to make a round trip to Bamberg for such strictly personal reasons is a subject best left unexplored. Even patriots sometimes diddle the system.

**The *Wehrmacht* did not choose its officer candidates on such a priori bases as pre-induction academic credentials or objective intelligence and personality tests. Commanders recommended men they considered suitable. These were then screened for background, including police and political records, and given a series of physical tests and psychologically focused interviews designed to determine not the intelligence, but the character of the applicant.

*   *   *   *   *

December 1939

Dear Father,

I am excited to be able to tell you that I will have a furlough after all, namely, the last week of December and the first week of January. I don't know how much you had to do with the sudden change of events, but I assure you that part of getting that furlough was my doing. Today we had our third exercise in shooting, prone position, distance 100 meters. I was the best shot in my platoon. By chance the first lieutenant came by and asked who the best shot was. "Tank gunner Fuchs, Sir" was the answer. "So," he said, "it's you. I challenge you, three shots, standing position, 100 meter distance. If you get more points than I, you can take your vacation early. Let's begin." The entire platoon stood around us and watched. I had to shoot first, and I knew that I could only win if I steadied my nerves because our first lieutenant is an excellent shot. I raised my gun, took a deep breath but still shook a bit. First shot, 9 points; second shot, 10 points; third shot, 12 points; 31 point total. Not bad, I thought, but will it be enough? Now it was his turn. First shot, 9 points; second shot, 11 points. He looked at me and smiled. I thought, "My God, I hope the last one isn't a bull's-eye!" Then came his third shot—10 points, one point fewer than I. My buddies celebrated with me and the first lieutenant shook my hand. I took a deep breath and smiled. You see, Father, you can be proud of me. Now all of us will be together after Christmas, and then we can plan my engagement party. I am looking forward to this day at home. A hearty Sieg Heil!

Your loyal son, Karl

This incident illustrates the *Wehrmacht*'s ideal officer–man relationship in practice. Authority, particularly on the lower levels, depended on ability. An officer worthy of his commission lost no status by challenging an enlisted man to a contest involving soldierly skills. And a really sophisticated training officer would know when and how to lose such a contest. It may not have been accidental that the lieutenant's score was *exactly* one point lower than Karl's.

* * * * *

18 January 1940

Dear Father,

Thanks for your kind letter. I want to tell you right away that I didn't volunteer for the Air Force because I don't care for their twelve-year obligation.* So much for that.

I am not surprised that you are loaded with work at this time. Everyone is working a lot, but I think the main task** is still ahead of us. You and I know what this means. I know that we'll complete this task to everyone's satisfaction and that our enemies abroad can be certain of this.

Mother also wrote me a very nice letter. I guess when the two of us are away, Mother can be very sensible. Let's hope this is the case when we are home again. We could truly lead a pleasant life at home if everyone could live in harmony. Perhaps the future will bring us the much sought-after peace in our home. We have, of course, no assurance that we'll ever get home again.***

Here at the base, all is really hectic. Our training continues to move ahead at a rapid pace. We recruit reserve officer candidates have lots of instruction and classroom work with the company commander and the first lieutenant. Once this training is completed and we move out of here, we'll be assigned to Tank Regiment 36 which is presently based in Schweinfurt.**** I guess we'll just take what comes. No matter what happens, we will fulfill our duty.

Say, did my friend Ritsch from Ansbach get assigned to you? If that is true, please send that recruit many greetings from his old friend Karl!

We are supposed to have night training this week and I'm looking forward to it. Hope to hear from you soon. Sieg Heil!

Your loyal son, Karl

*All branches of the *Wehrmacht,* even during World War II, retained long-service career options, one of which Karl had been considering during his initial weeks of service.

**The "main task" is no doubt in reference to winning the war on all fronts.

***Numerous times in his letters Karl addresses the theme of the soldier away from home fighting for his loved ones. He suppressed his fear of death by frequently mentioning the certainty of his return. Pride, honor, and fatalism combine to form a Germanic attitude reminiscent of the *Nibelungen* saga.

****The German army of World War II, unlike the American, was recruited and replaced territorially. Whenever possible, recruits were trained in the depots of the units they were to join in the field and assigned to divisions drawing most of their men from the same region. The 36th Tank Regiment, with its sister regiment, the 35th, belonged at that time to the 4th Panzer Division, formed in 1938 in Military District 13 (northern Bavaria and eastern Württemberg).

*   *   *   *   *

20 January 1940

Dear Mädi,

It's snowing outside; as a matter of fact it's snowing so much this winter that it seems like "old man winter" is trying to catch up with what he missed doing last year! Even under this blanket of snow there is a promise of a new beginning, a promise of spring. Soon the snow will melt and underneath it, new, young life will sprout up. What will this new time bring for us? We really don't know but one thing is for sure: we will never lose the belief in our good fortune, no matter how difficult times will be in the future. All of us believe in a just victory and in peace. This peace will become a reality only if we fight for it. I don't believe in this report about an imminent offer of peace.* In my opinion, it's no more than a rumor. Of course, many people would like to believe it and would be very relieved and happy if peace did come about soon. In the meantime, the struggle continues. We'll fight to the end and must be victorious!

A fierce cold has gripped the landscape. In spite of the temperature, our German land remains white and pure. The two of us love our beautiful German Fatherland so much that we surely can make this small sacrifice of time.**

Love, Karl

*In the winter of the "phoney war," numerous peace rumors swept a Germany whose people were on the whole anything but enthusiastic at fighting another general war. (Cf. Marlis Steinert, *Hitler's War and the Germans*, trans. T. J. De Witt (Athens, Ohio, 1977), 59ff.)

**Karl expands the theme of dutiful separation into an outline for a novel at a later date.

* * * * *

21 January 1940

. . . I have been instrumental in forming a company choir as well as a small orchestra. Next Saturday I will have to come home to pick up my violin and some music since I have a couple days of furlough.

Is my friend Ritsch working for you now? If that's the case, he should be finished with his first week by now. I just can't believe how quickly time passes! It seems that it won't be very long before we'll be able to take a swipe at those gentlemen in England! Let's hope for the best.

I'll write to you again on your birthday. For the time being, Sieg Heil!

Your son, Karl

In this letter to his father, it becomes evident that Karl intends to keep his cultural and intellectual activities alive in the military. He is also keenly interested in the whereabouts of his friends and their progress in the military. Most of his friends came from his home town of Rosstal; some of them, including Ritsch, were buddies from prep school days in Schwabach.

*   *   *   *   *

9 February 1940

Dear Father,

. . . Today during inspection it was pretty cold; nevertheless, we performed our duties during inspection with great enthusiasm and were praised for our efforts and performance. It must have been a magnificent sight to see hundreds of tanks maneuvering in unison. All of us were dressed in black death's-head uniforms* for the very first time. It was a picture of unquestionable courage and military strength. We all hope that we'll be transferred to the front soon. That is our greatest wish!

It is understandable that our women don't understand this wish. Well, that cannot matter. That is how the female soul functions. Women do not understand anything about the necessary struggle of a man and, in the final analysis, this must be the highest and noblest goal: a man must prove himself in battle. This battle is not only an individual struggle but also a struggle for our family as well as our German people.**

Now to something very important. Mädi and I plan to marry at Easter time, but only if we can get an apartment by then. I hope this news doesn't shock you and that you and Mother will approve. Father, the reasons for this sudden decision are numerous: first of all, I am the last one with the name Fuchs in our family tree, and what the continuing war still has in store for us no one knows; furthermore, I want to make certain that my Mädi's future is secure; lastly, the two of us truly want to be alone because we are sick and tired of the continuing family strife.*** I hope you understand all of my reasons and that you have nothing against a wartime wedding. These thoughts are constantly on my mind while I'm doing my duty here. Believe me, sometimes it's not easy but our belief in the Fatherland will shape our faith.

For today and the future, a hearty Sieg Heil!

Your loyal son, Karl

*Death's-head uniform—The German armored forces adopted a black uniform for no more sinister reason than in the color's relative tolerance for grease spots. The death's-head collar patches also owed nothing to National Socialism, but they harked back to the use of similar insignia by several famous Hussar regiments of the Imperial Army and reinforced the Panzers' self-image as "death-and-glory boys."

**The emphasis on battle as the ultimate test of manhood became increasingly widespread in the Weimar Republic, whose youth were legally forbidden the direct experience of military service that had modified the impact of popular militarism under the Empire. It also echoes themes from medieval Germanic sagas glorified in Wagnerian operas. Another point worth raising, though difficult to prove, is that Karl's patriotism is partly instrumental; a way of influencing his nationalist father. Karl's enthusiasm for defending his country tends to become effusive in direct ratio to his desire to bring his father to his point of view.

***Karl refers to disagreement about the kind of wedding he and Mädi were to have. In the 1930s the Nazis launched a campaign encouraging Germans to end their formal church membership. Hans Fuchs, as a prominent local Nazi, wanted a party wedding. Mädi, a Catholic, wished to be married in church—not only for religious reasons, but because the unfamiliar, improvised party ritual did not seem festive enough. Karl, in Bamberg, felt caught between two determined people whose conflict implied far more for his future than a choice of wedding forms.

* * * * *

14 February 1940

Dear Mother,

I received your parcel today and want to thank you for it. I am sorry to hear that you're not feeling well. Believe me, I can understand that you are sad now since Father has been transferred from Fürth, but you simply have to endure this hardship like a brave, German woman. You wrote that your only wish is for peace and I, as your son, can understand this completely. I am sure that other people are wishing for the very same thing. But whatever must be, must be.

I knew, of course, that you were in agreement with my marriage plans and I want to thank you for your trust. It's only a pity that you couldn't be with Mädi on her birthday. That certainly would have been a nice diversion for you.

Mother, please do one thing for me. Be kind enough and look through my papers for my birth certificate, my vaccination certificate and my certificate of Aryan ancestry.* Please don't forget this and take care of it as quickly as possible. It will facilitate the plans for our marriage.

Today we were vaccinated one more time. I am sore all over and am glad when I can lie in bed.

Greetings from your son, Karl

*The Fuchs family was able to trace its ancestry back 250 years, a great benefit in Nazi society.

*   *   *   *   *

17 February 1940

Dear Father,

. . . I'm glad to hear that you want to come and visit me on Sunday. I'm really looking forward to it because Mädi is also coming and then the three of us can discuss the most urgent issue, namely, our forthcoming marriage. I hope that you received my letter in which I explained my reasons for marrying Mädi. Mädi, in turn, spoke with Mr. Lehner, whom you know personally, and he promised her he would try to get her an apartment. Furthermore, Gustav* bought us a bedroom set; so you see we already have some furniture.

By the way, Mother invited the entire family and Mrs. Lehmann for Sunday. I wrote to her and explained that she had to be a brave German woman and shouldn't worry at all about the future. I hope that she takes my words to heart.

What is your opinion of this recent English pirate action? We will for sure teach those damn dogs a lesson and some manners!**

Well, good-bye until Sunday. I greet you with our old victory motto: Germany, Sieg Heil!

Your loyal son, Karl

*Mädi's father.

**Karl is most probably referring to the *Altmark* incident. This ship, loaded with British prisoners taken by the *Graf Spee*, was boarded in Norwegian territorial waters by HMS *Cossack* on 16 February. This technical violation of Norwegian neutrality, with its implications for future British behavior, led Hitler to expedite his plans for the seizure of Scandinavia.

* * * * *

28 February 1940

Dear Mother,

   In your last letter you brought up a subject that seems to be of some concern to you, namely, my marriage and my future children. Believe me, I know what I'm doing, I mean my fiancée and I are doing the right thing. Our children should be raised with the belief in our Fatherland! That too is a religion and the good Lord surely won't condemn that. It is the same whether we are Protestant or Catholic.* The main thing is that we live decent, respectable lives and that our children are reared properly, believing in one God in heaven.

   Now to something else. You shouldn't think now that Mädi's parents are well-to-do. You know that Mädi spent quite a bit of money studying at the university. The two of us need to save our money so that later on people won't say that we didn't contribute to our household. However, you and Father shouldn't expect my future in-laws, the Schoeppes, to plunk down 3,000 RM for furniture. They simply can't do that! That's another reason why there shouldn't be a great big party at our wedding. It is much more in order with the times to have a celebration with just a few of our friends in Rosstal. We are not quite sure yet whether or not we should have a church wedding. I think a civil ceremony would do. I am sure that you understand.

   Hearty greetings.

                                          Your loyal son, Karl

*Mädi was Catholic; Karl was a Protestant.

   An often-overlooked reason for Nazism's acceptability among educated young people was its official insistence that marriages between healthy Aryans should not be hindered by confessional values. Parental objection to Catholic-Protestant unions could now be challenged with the implied sanction of the government. Karl's rhetoric borrows heavily the Nazis' emphasis on *Gottgläubigkeit* as an alternative to traditional denominational adherence.

*   *   *   *   *

2 March 1940

Dear Mädi,

It's Saturday afternoon and I'm off-duty. This afternoon I had to clean up my area. Now all my comrades, with the exception of one, are gone. The remaining buddy and I are writing letters. For a change, a peaceful calm hovers over our barracks. The sun is shining through the windowpanes and the treetops are swaying in the March breeze. It is truly the right atmosphere for me to think of my good fortune.

When I sit down today and survey my life for the last year, it seems similar to the various parts of a symphony. Life first gave me anxious moments, then hope and finally the knowledge of your love. That's the way it was and that's why I would like to call this letter an overture to our lives. Listen and you will understand my composition.*

The earth is basking in brilliant sunshine. Quietly the swaying forests sing their song. A lonesome traveler is walking through nature, whistling a happy tune. In the distance you can hear the mysterious tune of an oboe; ascending cello and base chords provide a tender musical background. The bright flourish of a trumpet resounds and suddenly an echo of French horns is heard in the forest. The young man rejoices and in a brilliant tenor voice he answers the echo.** Now an echo of a thousand violins replies. He knows nothing of grief, sorrow and trouble in the world. He really doesn't know why he is so happy. Is it because of the beauty of nature? No, that isn't the only reason. Inside of him a feeling is awakening and this feeling starts to pound softly again and again. It is love, love for a human being with whom he became acquainted and this love makes his cheeks glow. The shadows become longer and the sun kisses the distant church towers. The church bells are quietly announcing the evening. This is my overture to love.

Another day. Two people sit on a forlorn bluff. The vast land in front of them is basking in sunshine and they look at each other silently. The song of love resounds once more, bright and pure and beautiful. The rich chords of the music sound wonderful but in the background you can hear the anguished sound of a trumpet. Can this love be without pain? Frequently these two people no longer know what they should do when they lie there sleeplessly. Suddenly, another trumpet signal, clear and audible. Fate calls to them with a brazen voice: "Why do you tarry? Don't I speak plainly enough? It is you who belong together. I brought you together and you had to travel on a difficult path at first so that you could know what love actually means, what it really means to love someone from the bottom of your soul!" The violins rejoice and the brass section of the orchestra resonates in this jubilation. At this point the man and woman hold hands. Their eyes shine brightly when they give each other rings as a sign of their faithfulness.

It is like a novel, just like each life is a novel. Once more the sound of trumpets is heard, but this time the sound isn't bright, pure and beautiful but rather jarring and metallic. The drums of war roll and without mercy tear the two loved ones apart. In anguish they depart. The man must fight and his bride must fear for his life. They have sworn to be faithful and loyal to each other. She is to help him get over the hardship and pain of war and she will do it. After all the fighting, after all the worrying, the sorrows, the longing and the hoping, the finale is played. A holy and beautiful ringing of bells announces peace and, amidst this ringing, they once more hold each other's hands. She, now relieved of all anxiety, embraces him with soft arms around his tanned neck. She sobs quietly and kisses him on the forehead. They walk on together into a future which for both of them will mean the greatest happiness. Yes, my dear, this is my novel and this is the way our life will be.***

Love, Korri

*The original German is highly romantic and stylized; alliteration and onomatopoeia abound.

**This is a theme from Carl Maria von Weber's opera, *Der Freischütz,* one of Karl's favorite musical compositions.

***The dream world of this romantic "novel" is kept alive until it ends one-and-a-half years later in the harsh reality of the desolate Russian landscape.

*   *   *   *   *

1 April 1940

My dear Parents,

This morning we moved our quarters. All of us officer candidates are together now and in a few days we'll be the only ones left in our company. It was a wonderful day! Outside the sun was shining brightly and almost the entire day was spent buzzing around with our tanks. Great!

I want to thank Mother for her nice letter. It alleviated a number of worries I had. It is not easy for a soldier to worry about things at home when he is doing his duty here. I agree with Mother completely that in the future we should only have peace and happiness in our family. Mädi, as my future wife, does belong to our family now and I have to tell you again and again what a wonderful person she is, even though she might be somewhat stubborn at times.

In the next weeks we are going to be taught to drive practically every kind of vehicle there is in the army and I will get a driver's license.* I guess that's important since I want to drive you around the countryside once I'm out of the army.

Yes, when you know that your home is peaceful and serene, then you are much happier away from home. Now it's time to hit the sack. In my thoughts I am with you.

Your thankful son, Karl

*The German army depended heavily on horse transportation throughout the war. It is an indication of the relatively low level of practical motorization in Hitler's Germany that a twenty-three-year-old tank crewman did not possess a driver's license.

*   *   *   *   *

9 April 1940

Dear Father,

What a day! What enthusiasm everywhere! German troops have marched into Denmark and Norway! What a depressing feeling that must be for those gentlemen in London and Paris. The "Huns" have done it again in good German style. And what are we doing here? We're sitting around at home like corralled horses and can only watch our comrades do our job. Believe me, many of us are becoming angry. We firmly believe, though, that our turn will come.

Last weekend at home certainly was wonderful! You could see how peace and quiet can make for a perfect weekend. I'm glad to see that Mother has become more reasonable about everything.

Tomorrow evening our small music combo will perform for Major Irmisch again. It's always very exciting and rewarding. I must rest up for Saturday, though, because that's the day for our examination in tank driving—practical and theoretical. Cross your fingers!

Hoping to hear from you soon, I remain

your loyal son, Karl
Sieg Heil!

*   *   *   *   *

17 April 1940

My dear Mother,

Today, after many anxious moments, I finally received my official permission to get married. Therefore, the marriage ceremony and the festivities will be next Thursday.*

Mädi wrote me the other day that you don't want to invite her girlfriends to the wedding. Mother, let's be reasonable! If you are going to invite half the town, doesn't it go without saying that Mädi can invite her friends? It won't make much difference, will it? After all, it is only polite that some of Mädi's acquaintances are present. It should be a pleasant day for all of us when your only child gets married!

I don't know exactly what time I'll be able to come home next week. At any rate, I'll be home by Wednesday at the latest. That also happens to be Mädi's father's birthday. I know that in your preparations for the festivities, you'll keep in mind that you love us.

Until Wednesday, many greetings from

your only son, Karl

*The wedding was a party ceremony, but more military than *völkisch*. Mädi and Karl left the town hall under an arch of swords and had an honor guard of Hans's "boys," former students in uniform and soldiers from his unit.

*   *   *   *   *

Rothenburg (Honeymoon postcard)

27 April 1940
Dear Father!
The "young Fuchs family" arrived in Rothenburg! We are very happy here. Fritz came along too to visit his relatives here, but I'm afraid he was totally smashed. He couldn't recollect a thing! Hail to victory.

Your loyal son, Karl

We are enjoying ourselves. The area is lovely. Hearty greetings, Mädi

*   *   *   *   *

Bamberg Army Base

5 May 1940
Dear Father,
After the wedding festivities I returned to the routine here at the base. Slowly but surely I'm becoming upset with the daily routine here and would like to get out and fight at the front. My comrades and I don't want to spend our entire military career here conducting dull training exercises. My God, we would like to accomplish something! We are tired of play-acting and are full of enthusiasm for battle. We didn't become soldiers to be treated like idiots. We should do something other than drill and instruction.*
All of these personal gripes become insignificant, though, when we hear news of victory at the front. Isn't it incredible what our troops, especially the Air Force, are achieving? Let me just mention the recent sinking of a British battleship with only one bomb! I feel sorry for the English, don't you? Slowly but surely

they are getting the picture over there on their island. I certainly wouldn't have wanted to be on that battleship. In the future people will say that the English rule the waves, but the Germans rule the air and control whatever happens to be floating in the water!**

I'm anxious to find out how things are going to develop in the south. I think that the Balkan powder keg will explode soon and if it does, England will certainly feel it too. I guess for us there is only one goal in this battle—to beat England on the water, on the land and, above all, in the air.***

My comrades here at the base presented me with a fabulous wedding present. It is a sculpture of the head of the famous Knight of Bamberg. I really like it.

Well, that's enough for today. Let me greet you with our old battle cry: Germany, Sieg Heil!

Your loyal son, Karl

*Under normal conditions, Karl's class of recruits would have been either dispatched as reinforcements to their parent units at the front or incorporated into new formations. Low casualties made the first alternative unnecessary; the lack of equipment made the second temporarily impossible.

**Heavy British losses to air attack in Norway included no battleships, but over-enthusiastic *Luftwaffe* reports were even more enthusiastically picked up and embellished by Goebbels.

***Karl's Anglophobia, a recurrent theme in his letters throughout 1940, partly reflects home conditioning based on his father's wartime experience. They also reflect Goebbels' bitter propaganda duel with Churchill in the winter and spring of 1940—and the fact that Karl was in no position to be exposed, as were so many of his *Volksgenossen,* to the BBC's broadcasts. (Cf. Robert Herzstein, *The War that Hitler Won: The Most Infamous Propaganda Campaign in History* (New York, 1978) 325ff.)

* * * * *

17 May 1940

My dear Mother,

Sunday, May 19th, is Mother's Day. In difficult times like these, the true meaning of Mother's Day becomes evident. How many thousands of mothers are anxious today and hope for the well-being of their sons! Yes, in these last couple of years, I have matured quite a bit and now know what I owe my Mother. I'm not the kind of person who can write a lot of pretty words, but on this day of honor for you I want to thank you for everything that you ever did for me and for all the things that you sacrificed for me. I will never forget that.

On this day I wish that you will be with us for many years to come and that sometime in the near future our children will be a source of great joy to you. Let's hope that all of us in our family will be able to spend many good times together. These are my wishes on Mother's Day. Greetings.

Your loyal son, Karl

P.S. During the next week I'll spend a couple of days in Rosstal and then it's off to the front!

Karl was a thoughtful and obedient child and even as a twenty-three-year-old would have never forgotten to remember his mother and father appropriately on special occasions.

*   *   *   *   *

19 May 1940
Dear Mädi,

I just heard the imposing sounds of the *Englandlied** over the radio. The whole base is excited. German soldiers have taken Saint Quentin! The German army is before the gates of Paris! It is wonderful what our soldiers are achieving! It is as if the old Teutonic spirit and the old strength of our forefathers are with them. Friedrich Barbarossa has arisen! He is with us in our fight against our archenemy. He leads us on to greater victories and soon to peace. And this Friedrich Barbarossa is none other than our Führer Adolf Hitler.**

Today we are proud. We can be proud to be German sons and daughters. Is it not a natural wish of all our people to present Germany with healthy children? Our love for each other is at the same time a love for our "Volk" and nothing should be more important to us than to devote our entire strength and all our efforts for this magnificent "Volk." If this is achieved, the two of us will also be able to live in peace.

Love, Korri

*The *Englandlied* (The England Song) by Hermann Löns (1866–1914) was a World War I fight song glorifying the naval forces. It became a popular Hitler Youth song during the Nazi period. The refrain encourages aggression towards England.

**On 10 May 1940, the *Wehrmacht* invaded France and the Low Countries. Karl's letter indicates the positive reactions of even the most cynical Germans to the speed with which the German army overran familiar landmarks of 1914–1918. The Germans were particularly impressed that the advances claimed few casualties. Karl's letter also shows how Goebbels' propaganda machine linked Hitler with virtually every hero of German antiquity. From the standpoint of social and family history, it might profitably be compared with letters of British and American newlyweds of World War II to their brides of less than two months. The preponderance of patriotic emotion contrasts sharply with the sentiments of the letter of 2 March.

* * * * *

Erlangen Army Base

2 June 1940

Dear Father,

We haven't heard anything from you in such a long time that we have reason to be worried.* Mother, in particular, is ill at ease. Yesterday Mädi sent me the letter which you had mailed to her. At least now I have a military postal number and can write to you.

From your letter it becomes evident that you were in the midst of things and that you once again saw all those battlefields which were so familiar to you from the Great War, battlefields which evoke German heroism and manliness. You were part of all the activity and I, your son, must sit here at home at the army base and wait. Dear Father, believe me, an incredible anger and sadness has gotten hold of us here. We so-called officer candidates seem to vegetate here at this base. Have we not completed our course work? I was transferred with two comrades to Tank

Regiment 25 in Erlangen.** It was explained to us officer candidates that all of us had to remain here and would not be sent to the front after all. This command, presumably, came right from the top. We tried everything to change their minds, but nothing helped. We had to stay, and they tried to appease us by telling us that we would certainly be part of the next transport to the front. This is supposed to be in eight weeks! Can you believe it? Naturally we want to try everything we can to get to the front and fight, but nothing seems to help. I almost don't dare to come home anymore because I am so ashamed. My God, had I volunteered for the Air Force when I had the chance, perhaps today I would be part of the fighting forces. This way you have the feeling the war will be over without any of us having fired a shot. Father, if anyone tags me a coward, I could not live with the shame!

My only pleasures in life are Mädi's visits. Father, she has become a dear friend and we understand each other so well since the wedding. Let me hear from you soon. I greet you with our old battle cry, Germany, Sieg Heil!

Your sad son, Karl

*Hans's unit provided communications for the *Luftwaffe* in the advance across France, and initially he was forbidden to write home for security reasons.

**The 25th Panzer Regiment had a complex history. Its life began as the 25th Panzer Battalion, a unit of the 2d Light Division, recruited from Karl's home military district (*Wehrkreis* 13). After the Polish campaign, the *Wehrmacht*'s light divisions were upgraded to Panzer formations. The 2d Light became the 7th Panzer Divison; the 25th Panzer Battalion expanded to a three-battalion regiment, equipped with Czech Pz 38 and Mark IV close-support tanks. Under Erwin Rommel, the division and the regiment would win fame in the 1940 campaign. (See Hasso E. von Manteuffel, *Die 7. Panzer-Division im Zweiten Weltkrieg* (West Germany: Krefeld, 1965), 22.)

*   *   *   *   *

5 June 1940

My dear Mother,

I received your letter and was pleased to hear the news about Father. Now, however, I must tell you something that will probably cause you great pain but that can't be helped. Next

Monday, June 10th, I'm off to the front.* I am looking forward to it; otherwise I wouldn't be a German. Just look at my brave comrades who have fought all this time, who have put their lives on the line for our Fatherland and our Führer. The first battle has taken place and ended in glorious victory.** This current battle has been raging for only a short time; yet these foreign culprits refused the peace offerings of our Führer. In a few weeks this struggle will also come to a victorious conclusion and in the fall the war will be over.

I know how difficult it is for you, Mother, and it also is hard on my young wife. You must understand that you women have to be as brave as those of us at the front. I know that I will return and there will be no more beautiful reunion than the one we will experience in peacetime. All of us are looking forward to this moment when the church bells will ring out "peace" across our great land.

All of us are ready to march. We have received new gear and new uniforms and things couldn't be better. Please say hello to all my friends in town and especially everyone in the house. Tell them I didn't have time to write to all of them. You, dear Mother, think of me when I am out there on the front fighting and be certain that I will always honor you as my good Mother.

Your loyal son, Karl

*Karl was proud to hear that his time had finally come. The order to move out, however, was rescinded several days later.

**The invasion of Poland.

* * * * *

Postcard from Nuremberg

6 June 1940

Dear Father,

I am spending the day with Mädi in Nuremberg. We are having dinner at the Königshof where we had so many good times. Tomorrow it's off to the front and on to battle and victory.

Your Karl

* * * * *

Dear Father,

Now Korri is also going to leave me. I will be all alone but I know that you both have to return! I know that for certain.

Greetings, Mädi

*   *   *   *   *

Erlangen Army Base

12 June 1940

My dear Mädi,

Are you listening to the radio? I just heard an announcement about the latest German victory. German troops only 20 kilometers from Paris!!* Of course, we aren't part of this and it looks like we're going to be too late anyway. You, my dear, must be happy and glad since you don't have to fear for my safety. Yes, the biggest victory has taken place! France has capitulated and peace is at hand. Don't worry, Mädi, because it doesn't look like we'll be called on to fight. Nevertheless, it's wonderful when you think about the great things our troops are doing. I firmly believe that this year we will celebrate the most fantastic party rally ever and perhaps by then I'll be out of the army. Who would have thought it? God in heaven led our magnificent Führer and our brave and loyal soldiers. Are you glad that I'm not in danger? I am somewhat saddened that I wasn't involved at all. Fate apparently ordered that I should be with you. I just hope that no one will call me a coward. I rejoice with you and the entire German nation. To our Führer a Sieg Heil!

Your Karl

*On 5 June the regrouped German armies struck south into France. By 10 June they had crossed the Somme. Paris itself was occupied on 14 June. Effective French resistance can be said to have ceased by the 15th or the 16th.

*   *   *   *   *

20 June 1940

Dear Father,

You could be proud of your only son if he had been part of Germany's most magnificent victories. Several weeks ago I told you that it was finally our turn to go to the front, but now nothing came of it. On 10 June our march unit* went to the front but without us. Orders from headquarters: All officer candidates have to remain here!! This time we weren't disappointed but enraged! We ran from officer to officer and finally to the commander, explaining to them that we would renounce all claims to becoming officers if we only got to go. All of our attempts were in vain. While we told them that we wanted to volunteer right away for the paratroopers, they asked us: "Gentlemen, aren't you proud of your tank unit?" Obviously, they were trying to call upon our loyalty. Apparently our division is in dire need of young officers, much more so than any other division.** We have become pessimists and believe that we will never get to go to the front— not even to take revenge on England.

Oh Father, had I listened to you and gone into the Air Force, I would have been part of the action long ago. I am ashamed in front of you and all my comrades. You are a part of the action and I, the son of an old soldier, am banished to the hinterland. The war will be over and I won't have had a chance to do anything for our Führer or for our Fatherland. Perhaps my chance is yet to come.

Please write and console me.

Your sad son, Karl

*Standard German practice was to dispatch reinforcements in organized provisional formations, rather than to send individual replacements or ad hoc detachments.

**The need for officer candidates was caused in part by losses in the French campaign, and partly by a reaction to Rommel's high standards for command, which by this time had permeated his division to company and platoon levels.

* * * * *

25 June 1940

Dear Mother,

Now that the war between Germany and France is over, my dear wife has a day off from school. She drove to Erlangen this morning and now we're sitting here alone. My departure from the base has been delayed until Thursday morning. They told us that we're going to be stationed near Versailles.* So you see, you won't have to fear for my safety after all because the war with France is over. It is possible that when we leave on Thursday we will be routed through Seuckendorf. If you want to give Mädi a short letter for me, she can perhaps slip it to me as we drive through the village. Believe me, when I return I will bring all of you a little present and I'm certain that my return will be only a matter of weeks. When I return we will celebrate and I know that this festivity will be the most beautiful time in our lives.

Please don't be sad, but be proud of me. Greetings from your son.

Karl

*Prior to his tour of duty in France, Karl had never left his native Germany. As a fifteen-year-old boy, he had taken a train trip down the Rhine Valley and on to Hamburg, visiting acquaintances and relatives. Two years later, in the summer, a journey to Leipzig-Weimar followed. During the Olympic summer of 1936, he took an extended bicycle-camping trip to the North Sea. As a harvest helper in the Labor Service, he had been to the Czech border. Entering a foreign land and enemy territory was, for Karl, no doubt an adventurous undertaking. He was probably aware, though, as a university-educated teacher, of the educational benefits of such a trip.

*   *   *   *   *

Paris

7 July 1940

Dear Mädi,

I've been away from home now for almost two weeks and have seen and experienced a lot. I have become acquainted with many French customs and traditions.

For the time being we have our quarters set up in a wonderfully situated château. The architecture of the château is similar to an old Roman villa. In front of the château there's an oval-shaped pond and beyond the pond is a lush forest. The château is situated on a small hill from which you can look far out into the countryside, almost as far as Paris. It is a superb location! I'm sure that my little wife would like to be here as well.

Here in this old democracy, you sense the tremendous difference between the rich and the poor: on the one hand, there are palaces (but even here you no longer have the feeling of cleanliness); on the other hand, there are huts full of poverty.

I've been standing guard since noon today, not in front of this château but in front of another aristocratic piece of property. It's also a château but belongs to an American. The grounds surrounding it are most splendid!

Life in a strange land is interesting for a while, but it's not beautiful like home. If you could take a trip through the countryside, your first impression would be favorable, I'm sure; but staying for a long time in the same place without the one you love is a most boring existence.

Love, Karl

*   *   *   *   *

7 July 1940

Dear Mother,

I've seen quite a bit of France so far and have experienced some new things, but again and again I say to myself that there's nowhere as beautiful and clean as our great German Fatherland!*

The stream of French refugees has diminished and most of them are back in their old villages or cities. Only once in a while do you see a two-wheeled cart with refugees on the street. Otherwise, it's quite peaceful on the streets, traffic is normal and France seems to be calm.

The French civilian population is quite polite to us; of course, they know who we are! For the time being, we're stationed in a rather large château. As far as the landscape is concerned, it's most beautiful and I really can't complain.

How are you, dear Mother? I suppose you feel rather lonely but all of this will soon be over. We believe that we'll be home in a matter of weeks. We're all certain that England won't be able to hold out much longer and it's just a matter of whether or not we'll be part of the invasion. I suppose you have to take things as they come.

I haven't heard anything from Father. I hope that you told him how to get in touch with me so he can write to me.

Be cheerful and look to the future with optimism because all of the waiting will soon be over. Greetings and Sieg Heil!

Your loyal son, Karl

*Karl's attitude, "there's no place like home," is worth highlighting because of its frequent occurrence in German soldiers' letters from both world wars, and because of its similarity to the opinions of American servicemen stationed outside their own country.

* * * * *

West of St. Germain, France

15 July 1940

Dear Mädi,

Today I bought this exquisite stationery in Versailles for a reasonable price. We were driven to the French Potsdam today in order to visit the château and the park of Versailles. It was a pity that all the rooms had been emptied of all artifacts, but the French government had removed them for safe keeping. Even without them, you could get a picture of a former opulent French culture. For instance, paintings on the ceilings of many rooms were framed in pure gold! It was a shame that we didn't have enough time to carefully examine all these pictures. I especially liked a wonderful marble chapel with a magnificent organ. Then we came to that well-known Hall of Mirrors where the fate of Germany had been decided twice before, once in 1871 in favor of German power and unity, and the other time after the Great War to bring about the deepest humiliation of the German people. It's a rather strange feeling for a young German to stand here and let the history of the last seventy years pass by. Many of us were also impressed by the so-called Gallery of Battles in which famous French generals, among them Napoleon I, were depicted.*

When we entered the sleeping quarters of the powerful Sun King, King Louis XIV, we could almost breathe the air of numbing sultriness of the time. Here in these quarters you could imagine what decadent debauchery this most famous French king was engaged in with that Pompadour woman. This is the air that

France still breathes today. Life seems to be devoted to passion alone.

Later my soldier-friends and I went to a "bookstore" in Versailles. You can't imagine what junk and pornography we saw! There were nothing but magazines full of erotic pictures. The shopkeeper kept saying, "Oh messieurs, très bien," in order to get us to buy some of these books. We, however, had only one answer: "No, monsieur, très mal." You can truly see that in the areas of cleanliness and morality, the French people have skidded to a new low. Such an incident is simply unthinkable and impossible in our German Fatherland. When a society is capable of reducing the feminine beauty to such a level, then this society has lost its right to be called a "grande nation." Yes, this society has lost not only its vitality but also its morality.**

Love, Korri

*Karl's division was on occupation duty west of St. Germain. As part of a program designed to keep garrison forces busy and, at the same time, to convince the French that their conquerors were not savages, the *Wehrmacht* organized regular tours of cultural centers. It also insisted on high standards of behavior for men on pass or furlough—standards generally fulfilled, to the surprise of many Frenchmen.

**Karl was not merely writing to impress his new bride with his high moral standards. Like many Germans brought up between the wars, he had accepted and internalized a sharp distinction between healthy sensuality and "decadent" eroticism.

$$*\quad*\quad*\quad*\quad*$$

Rochefort, near Paris

21 July 1940

Dear Father,

I've finally received your new address. Six weeks ago when we left home rather hastily, I forgot to get your new military postal number from Mädi. Thus we've not been able to communicate with each other for about a month. Since then, great things have happened in the history of Germany but precious little has happened to me!

You remember, of course, that when we were sent to France

several weeks ago, the Armistice was already in effect. We had hoped to get at least as far as England, but our hopes are going to be dashed again.* I no longer believe that I'll have the opportunity to fight at the front. I've had such bad luck in this war and what are the consequences? No one around here is getting promoted. What good is it to be here in France? I see absolutely no merit to our being here. We are treated just like we were back at the army base in Erlangen; sometimes things are even worse than when we were recruits.

How are things with you and where are you? You, as an old frontline soldier, have experienced much more in this war than your young son. That is the irony of fate. Actually I should be ashamed, but it really isn't my fault, is it? The one mistake I made a year ago was not enlisting in the Air Force. But who could have known that then? Here in France I'm also enrolled in an officer candidate course since none of the courses which I took at home are accepted here! After all these frustrating and unfair experiences, I simply don't have my heart in my work anymore. Instead, I could be home advancing in my teaching profession . . . . Sieg Heil!

Your loyal son, Karl

*From mid-August to the end of October, the 7th Panzer Division was preparing and exercising for Operation Sea Lion, the aborted invasion of Britain.

By this time Hans Fuchs has been assigned as *Stadtkommandant* of Saint Cloud—a rear-area post he considered highly uncongenial. There were, of course, many cultural and social benefits. Because of his musical ability, particularly piano playing, and his competency in French, Major Fuchs had no difficulty making acquaintances.

* * * * *

31 July 1940

Dear Mädi,

Last night some of my comrades and I sat in our room and celebrated. The reason for the celebration was the awarding of the Iron Cross, Second Class, to some of the guys in our unit. They told us of the war since some of them have been at the front.

Indeed, they earned this honor. One of them is from Ammerndorf, halfway between Rosstal and Cadolzburg. You know the town and I know him from former days in the Hitler Youth. We have a great unit here and all of us get along so well. Naturally, champagne was needed to properly celebrate this occasion!

Today we roared through the region in our tanks, mostly through the forests. These French forests are somewhat strange and appear to be a huge wilderness full of magnificent chestnut and beech trees and ferns which are rather tall and thickly scattered. This place is entirely surrounded by forested ridges and from the top you can look down on St. Germain and also see the hidden villas and châteaux. Let me tell you, these French "money men" spend an unbelievable amount of money on their magnificent living quarters. This clique certainly understood how to live in comfort and pleasure.*

Yesterday I had to clean the room of our Sergeant Major. It was my turn. Our present quarters are very comfortable but compared to "his" château with its medieval decor, ours seem shabby. From the outside these houses don't impress you that much, but as soon as you cross the threshold, you can sense this French opulence. Naturally, there is quite a bit of kitsch included which doesn't surprise me, but in general these villas and châteaux are magnificently decorated. All the floors are covered with expensive rugs which cushion every step you take, making the sound of your walking almost inaudible. Naturally, a bar is included in the dining room. Almost every room seems to have a built-in bath. The beds are much wider than ours at home and are covered with expensive bedspreads. Unlike the two single side-by-side beds that we're accustomed to, the French have just one large bed, which is in keeping with their sultry lifestyle.** You can generally say that all these châteaux have one thing in common: they all seem to ooze an oppressive sultriness which intoxicates the senses. I guess that just fits the erotic lifestyle of the French. In France you can find incredible contrasts: opulent wealth on the one hand and poverty, filth and lice on the other. My conviction remains the same—there's only one Germany! Mädi, you can't imagine how often we speak of the Fatherland! What a marvelous feeling it will be when we cross the German border again and breathe the air of our homeland. I know that at that moment, I'll have tears of joy and relief in my eyes.

With all my love, Your Karl

*Another passing indication that the "socialist" element of National Socialism could have significant rhetorical impact on Germans of Karl's generation. Though the Nazi revolution quickly stagnated, its vision of an ideologically based *Volksgemeinschaft* endured through 1945, and might be said to flourish currently in the rhetoric of the German Democratic Republic. (Cf. Michael Kater, *The Nazi Party: A Social Profile of Members and Leaders, 1919–1945* (Cambridge, Mass., 1983); and David Childs, *The GDR: Moscow's German Ally* (London, 1983).)

**To this day in rural small-town Germany, mention of a *französisches Ehebett* or *französisches Doppelbett* can evoke smirks, blushes and giggles in certain company.

Karl's platoon is now comfortably stationed in a villa near St. Germain—the food is to their liking and they "devour delicacies every day." His father's post is only a few kilometers away and they communicate regularly. Karl's greatest concern at this time is that he still has not been promoted to corporal. His hope is that he'll be able to prove himself in the anticipated England invasion.

*   *   *   *   *

St. Germain

3 August 1940

Dear Father,

. . . There is the distinct possibility, actually it seems like a 99% certainty, that we're still going to cross the Channel.* If that happens, I'll be ready to give my all. At any rate, the days are numbered for these bums over there in England. They won't be able to attack German cities and peaceful farms anymore. All of us feel that once we're over there, no one will show any mercy whatever, no matter who's involved. All those bums are the same. If fate sends me over there, I'm going to fight until I keel over! Thank God that I am now the commander of a large tank. At least that's a step in the right direction.

Our group is really a terrific fighting unit and we all stick together. Most of the guys are from Nuremberg and the surrounding villages. For instance, Michael Müller from Ammerndorf is an old friend of mine from the Hitler Youth. He has already been in sixteen attacks and as a reward for his bravery at the front, he received the Iron Cross. He's a great guy. And yesterday I met a man from Rosstal named Michel Meth. He's in the regimental band but has also participated in several earlier attacks. As you can imagine, we emptied a couple of bottles while we celebrated meeting each other. This just goes to show that the people of Rosstal are everywhere.** If we are called upon to fight, none of us will quit fighting until every English dog over there has stopped barking! We're confident that we will finish them off.

Fighter planes and bombers are just heading north over our heads. I suppose that in a few days we'll march in that direction too—you up there in the air and I down here on the ground. Let's hope that we'll see each other again and that we'll both stay healthy. Our battle cry as always is Germany, Sieg Heil!

Your loyal son, Karl

P.S. I sent a couple of parcels with silk garments to Mädi.

*Karl seems to have been repeating latrine rumors here—rumors perhaps encouraged by the growing intensity of the air battle over England, whose signs were increasingly apparent in northern France.

**This point illustrates again the value of the *Wehrmacht*'s emphasis on regional ties in recruiting and reinforcing its formations. The original north Bavarian character of the 25th Panzer Regiment steadily changed, however, because the 7th Panzer Division was assigned to District 9, Thuringia, as a replacement area on its formation.

* * * * *

Near Paris

16 August 1940

My one and only Mädi,

Another day has gone by, a day with few pleasures, a day gray and monotonous. I frequently become dejected and ask myself why I am here. What is there to gain from the constant drill in the courtyard, from superiors always screaming "about face" and the like? With every passing day, the activity here resembles basic training more and more.

Today we were told what will be in store for us in the next few weeks. It seems certain that we'll sit around here until a peace treaty is signed. No one knows how far I will have progressed by then but one thing is for sure—I am slowly but surely going insane! Mädi, just try to imagine what it means for an intellectual person to perform the same routine every day. This monotonous existence is beyond me. My God, why don't they send us to England?

You will recall with what idealism and enthusiasm I joined the military nearly a year ago. Well, that's enough of that. One of these days this period of my life will be over and then I'll only recall the enjoyable hours of comradery. I have been a soldier for nine months and I'm not even a corporal. This is a disgrace for me, but I can't do anything about it. I definitely wanted to go to the front and fight and never dreamed that I'd be a member of the Occupational Forces in enemy territory.

Love, Your sad Korri

In the aftermath of the Battle of France, some German divisions were in fact temporarily demobilized, their conscript personnel made available to an economy already badly short of labor. The elite Panzer forces were not merely kept intact, but expanded. The number of divisions was doubled in 1940–1941, though the number of tanks in each was reduced by as much as half.

*   *   *   *   *

23 August 1940

Dear Father,

On Monday as I was driving back from your quarters, I picked up a letter carrier. He told me that the British fighter planes don't even have the courage anymore to attack the German planes.* Up until now, at least in my opinion, the British Air Force has only tasted the German attacking spirit! What are they going to do when, instead of 200 planes, 1,000 start to attack? Well, we here can do nothing but wait. We're good at that! That just goes to show how disciplined the German soldier is!!**

I sure hope we can work out something about my furlough. It's not that I'm anxious to go home soon, but rather that I've got the chance to fly home with you. You know, I've lately become interested in flying again. Even if I did join the Air Force, though, there would be no assurances that I would become a member of the active forces right away.

I received a very nice letter from Mother today with some cigarettes enclosed. Apparently she had visited with the in-laws. Gustav, however, was in Berlin at the time. It seems that all three women slept in one bed in Nuremberg! Who knows what they talked about. The important thing is that Mädi's mother told Mother that Gustav really isn't Mädi's father. Mother apparently said that it didn't make any difference at all and that she liked Mädi and the in-laws just as much as before. Well, it certainly wouldn't have made any difference to the two of us. You and I have never placed much importance on superficialities, but have always considered and scrutinized the inner man. At any rate, Mother believes that Mädi is the right wife for me and feels that she loves me very much. I'm anxious to see how things will be when the two of us return home again.

A couple of days ago we officer candidates once again were the guests of our company commander. It was very nice. Unfortunately the commander was depressed since he had heard through the grapevine that the Air Force will carry out the major attacks against England. We'll see. Nevertheless, we're all ready; no matter what orders come, they will be carried out. That's why we are soldiers.

I hope your next letter comes soon. I'm also anxiously awaiting your arrival here and then the flight home. For today I greet you with our old battle cry, Germany, Sieg Heil!

Your loyal son, Karl

P.S. I would like to request one thing from you. Do you suppose that you could find some silk pajamas for Mädi?*** Naturally, I'll pay for it. Do what you can.

---

*This cavalier judgment expressed by a groundhog in the presence of German air crews might well have cost its author a few teeth. Heavy casualties combined with the continued fierce resistance of RAF Fighter Command led in fact to the decision to switch the emphasis to urban industrial targets. The first planned attack on London came on 24 August.

**On very few occasions, a note of cynicism creeps into Karl's letters.

***This reference calls to mind Bertolt Brecht's 1942 poem "And What Did the Soldier's Wife Get?"

* * * * *

1 September 1940

Dear Mädi,

I just finished washing the dishes and am now doing my weekly laundry. My pants and shirts are hanging on the clothesline outside, flapping in the fall breeze. Yes, that's correct, the fall breeze. Today is the first of September and by this time we wanted to be home again—I mean for always. But who can say how long we're going to stay here? Maybe we'll even have to go to England! Who knows?

The September sun is scorching hot and the sky is a deep blue. The air, however, is filled with the thunder and roar of German bombers, Stukas and fighter planes. All are headed towards England, the archenemy. Only a little while ago some of us were talking about receiving our marching orders to move over there. We have no choice but to wait, even though it is very difficult for us. Apparently the time is not yet ripe to reap the harvest which the German air heroes have sown. The time will come, though, and it will be a pitiless and dreadful time for England.

Yesterday we actually visited Paris. You have to admit that it's a grandiose city with its wonderful boulevards with beautiful views. No doubt, the most beautiful view was the one from the royal château, from those blood-soaked Tuileries through the small Arc de Triomphe of Napoleon, past the Obelisk to the large Arc de Triomphe up the boulevard. You know that the small Arc de Triomphe of Napoleon is the one on which the four horses from the Brandenburg Gate once stood. Today there's only a copy there. The Obelisk is a structure which Napoleon brought back from his Egyptian campaign. It's very impressive! Right out of the midst of Paris grows the Eiffel Tower, a magnificent structure of iron. We climbed up approximately a thousand steps and that was exhausting! Our knees started to get weak and shaky. From this dizzying height you have an exceptional view of the metropolis of Paris. Right at the foot of the Eiffel Tower is the

World Exposition area; the parks and the modern buildings, among which is the Trocadero Theatre, are quite nice. Others, however, are too modern in their architectural style to fit into the environment. The Dome of the Invalides in which Napoleon is buried and the Pantheon, some sort of hall of fame like our Walhalla, are enormous, just like Notre Dame Cathedral. But I was most impressed by the Sacre Coeur Church which is built in the style of a mosque. This church overlooks Paris from its hillside location and is truly impressive.

Life itself in Paris is back to normal. I must say, though, the most terrible sights are the Negroes who walk arm-in-arm with white French women and who sit with them in the street cafes. I just can't approve of that!*

In the evening we drove back to the base in our trucks because none of us were allowed to stay and go shopping in Paris. We're prohibited from walking alone through Paris. One more nice thing is that in front of the headquarters of the German army in France there were two guards and around them approximately a hundred Frenchmen. They stood there and just stared at the guards. Apparently they had never seen anything like this before—I mean, they had seen guards but not this kind of guard. The two Germans, who looked like they were cast in bronze, stood there with rifles ready. Nothing moved, not a muscle or an eyelid! It was a wonderful picture of genuine German soldiership. My comrades and I felt proud when we saw them.

Well, so much for Paris.

Love and kisses, Korri

---

*Apart from generalized racism, German nationalists had been particularly sensitized on the issue by the regular presence of French North African troops in the Rhineland occupation forces during the 1920s and 1930s. Allegations of rape—almost all unfounded—played a significant role in Nazi propaganda. Many of the mixed-blood children these men left behind were sterilized in the 1930s. (Cf. Sally Marks, "Black Watch on the Rhine: A Study in Propaganda, Prejudice, and Prurience," *European Studies Review 13* (1983), 297–334; and Reiner Pommerin, "The Fate of Mixed Blood Children in Germany," *German Studies Review 5* (1982), 315–23.)

*   *   *   *   *

7 September 1940

Dear Mädi,

I too have a bit of news for you! Yesterday I was promoted to corporal!* Aren't you amazed? I see this promotion as an acknowledgement of all the hard work that I've done. Yet, this promotion is a matter of total indifference to me. Whatever may come, I do what I have to and what my sense of duty requires me to do—no more.

Father was here yesterday and it was very nice to talk to him. Now he wants to fly home on the 13th or 14th of September. Father and I also stopped by to see the Company Commander and Father asked him whether or not I might be permitted to fly home with him. Unfortunately I have to tell you that there doesn't seem to be much hope at the moment about coming home. Let me tell you why. At the moment the military situation around here is rather touch-and-go. You yourself must have heard on the radio that everything is prepared for the decisive battle, especially after our bombings are now not only hitting military targets in England but also London itself. I guess it's about time that London was hit anyway. Any furlough has been cancelled and nothing can be changed as far as these decisions are concerned.**

Dear Mädi, I beg you to be strong and not to make me long for you more by writing in your next letter that you miss me terribly. Think of the thousands who also cannot come home and of those thousands of women who are in your situation. Last but not least, think of our Fatherland and our Führer to whom we give everything as his children. The fate of all German people is at stake. We simply have to sacrifice and I know that we can do it. I miss you terribly but I know the day will come when we will be united in happiness once again.

Love and kisses, Your Karl

*Until actually commissioned, a German officer candidate went through the junior noncommissioned grades like everyone else. Promotion, however, was not only desirable for its own sake—a corporal had to do less of the dirty work—but was an indication of eventual fitness for officer's rank. This is why promotions, or lack of them, appear so frequently in Karl's letters.

**A precautionary measure taken at divisional level in possible preparation for *Sea Lion*.

*   *   *   *   *

2 October 1940

Dear Mädi,

I'm in a terrible mood! I just completed the most ridiculous and monotonous writing assignment in all my life! I had to write thirty times, "I am not permitted to forget anything and I am not allowed to come late!" Isn't that something? I am so mad I could scream! I wrote to you that I'm now taking a course for noncommissioned officers. Because of something stupid that happened in this class, I had to complete this childish punishment. I am the last one who would complain about military drills, but I can't stand this harassment. Naturally, drill is part of the military and every German soldier knows that he never complains no matter how often he has to hit the deck during morning workouts, or has to run up and down the field until his tongue hangs out of his mouth or until his uniform is wet from the moist grass. No one complains about that, but what I have always fought against and could never stand is injustice. I hate injustice just as much as I despise unfaithfulness. I tell you, after you have hit the ground 50 or 60 times just because a superior officer has a bone to pick with you, then you really lose your temper.

During my free time I have taken it upon myself to arrange a few musical evenings for the soldiers. You know how much I love doing that! Well, our music was well received and I think we created a few entertaining evenings. What kind of a reward is it, however, when you get nothing but thanklessness, annoyance and, indeed, harassment for all your hard work? I really tried with these musical evenings to provide a little diversion from the day-to-day monotony and to create a fun, carefree atmosphere. My efforts, though, are not appreciated and I've lost all interest in ever arranging an evening like this again. I am becoming disgusted with this kind of life. I want to do something, create something. I also want to get some recognition for the extra work which I put in and don't want to be thought of as an idle idiot. Just

try and speak with your superior officer about something important, just once, and the first thing he'll say is to shut up! I hope my
present frustration will soon pass.* Until then,

Love and kisses, Your Korri

*Karl's frustrations apparently came about when his artistic efforts
collided with an intransigent bureaucracy.

*   *   *   *   *

9 November 1940

Dearly beloved Mädi,

It's November and gray fog covers the earth as the rain falls
quietly. The last words of the Führer's radio address are over and
new strength streams through our veins. It is as if he spoke to
each individual, to everyone of us, as if he wanted to give
everyone new strength. With loyalty and a sense of duty, we must
fight for our principles and endure to the end. Our Führer
represents our united German Fatherland. He also represents the
smallest segment of this union and that is marriage, German
marriage. What we do for him, we do for all of you; what we
sacrifice in foreign lands, we sacrifice for all of you loved ones.
When the Führer speaks during these festive occasions, I feel
deep in my soul that you at home also feel that we must be ready
to make sacrifices.

All of our sacrifices will be rewarded when the last enemy
has been conquered with irresistible force. German victory is as
certain as our love for each other. Just as we believe in our love,
so do we believe in our final victory and in the future of our
people and our Fatherland. Our Fatherland's future is but the
future of our children. And we will have a child, a strong boy or a
lovely girl—that doesn't matter—and we'll build a future for this
child, a future that is beautiful and worthy of life. It is our most
holy duty and our most beautiful assignment to fight and struggle
for this future. It is worthy of every sacrifice we can make.*

Love, Korri

*This mixture of patriotism and domesticity may seem incongruous to a
contemporary reader, but Frau Fuchs-Richardson affirms its deep impact when she received it.

*   *   *   *   *

10 November 1940

Dear Father,

Once again it's Sunday. Instead of being at home on furlough, I'm sitting here in the community room, listening to the
German radio hour. At least that's a touch of home.

Last night we all listened to the speech of our Führer. All I
can say is that it was magnificent and overwhelming. Yes, it really
feels good to hear our Führer speak again and indeed have him
speak to each one of us. Suddenly you understand why you are
here in a foreign land and why you have to wait. You feel the
greatness and the intensity of our times and all the monotony of
everyday life somehow disappears. Now only one thing matters
and that is our German Fatherland.

In the meantime, my officer candidate course at the regiment
continues. It seems that we are starting all over again. By the
way, my fellow officer candidate Prückner, whom I introduced to
you, was promoted to sergeant a week ago. Of course I thought to
myself, "Why did it happen to him and not to me?" Apparently
the decision was based on the fact that he is an active officer
candidate while I am a reserve officer candidate. He and I had the
best grades during the noncommissioned officer's course. My
superior at the moment, Lt. Müller, is of the opinion that these
promotions always take longer for reservists. That's all very well,
but I really wanted to be a sergeant when I come home for
Christmas.*

Mädi wrote me that she was terribly sad that I couldn't
come. However, she was enthused about your nice letter. It
seems that Mother and Mädi want to get ready for the baby by
doing some knitting. For that they need wool and for the life of
me, I can't find any to buy. I also wanted to buy some brown
boots, size 38, for Mädi. Since you have some connections, I
would like to ask you whether you could try to find those items. I
would really appreciate it if you could help me find these gifts.

Mother wrote to me and was excited about all your presents.
Suddenly she is speaking of a new happiness, the likes of which
she hasn't felt before. Hope to hear from you soon. Sieg Heil!

Your loyal son, Karl

*Here again Karl was feeling the effect of a problem not generally associated with Hitler's *Wehrmacht;* too many men qualified for too few command slots. The 25th Panzer Regiment's commander, Colonel Rothenburg, was himself too much the *alte Hase* to release these enthusiastic youngsters to other formations. Instead he risked having them go stale through repetition, knowing they would be needed in the coming campaign against Russia. The regiment's brilliant performance in Operation Barbarossa owed much to its constantly renewed corps of junior leaders.

*   *   *   *   *

11 November 1940

My darling Mädi,

Now I want to outline for you the plot of our novel as I would like to write it. Listen to me—this is the way it should begin. There are two students in their third semester, students in the dreamy, romantic city of Würzburg, two human beings, a happy young girl and a young man full of vitality. Both have experienced much in their lives and yet, both of them have been disappointed by life as well. They know nothing of each other. They only know that they are friends. The young man experienced some time ago that a woman's love and loyalty are all for naught and he can no longer believe in love; the young girl, however, does believe that she has found the right man at last. Fate now enters the lives of these human beings and whispers into the ear of the lonely man that this happy, beautiful, young woman is truly his right comrade for life. This is the theme of my novel and it is our task to tell this tale in truthful, sincere words. Help me so that I may succeed.

Korri

*   *   *   *   *

24 November 1940

Dear Father,

. . . When you are young, inexperienced and get married, sometimes there are things that are best kept to yourself and that's the way it was with this Polish situation. I actually intended to volunteer for duty there and had made up my mind to teach in the reacquired Polish territory.* Your assumption that I did this because I am dissatisfied with my present military assignment is correct. I also volunteered for this position out of pure idealism. Lastly, you must remember that I coincidentally received at that time a letter from the Superintendent of Schools, pointing out to me the attractiveness of such a position. At no time did I intend to go to Poland to teach in order to avoid military service. You are correct, however, when you say that some other people could have interpreted my move to Poland as just that. Well, to make a long story short, I did not volunteer for a teaching assignment in Poland because I realized that it would be pointless. . . .

. . . When you notice how other comrades are already going home on furlough for the second time and you yourself have to watch them leave and don't even know when or if you'll get your turn, then you really want to say to your superiors, "You can cram your eternal lectures and courses up your you-know-what!" If we were only at the front fighting, then all of these matters would be much easier to take. This endless waiting and the uncertainty of the future are really nerve-racking. Frequently my friends and I stand outside of our bunker and look up to see our fighter planes flying north. Then we all wish that we too could be engaged in battle. You damn guys in the Air Force apparently want to do it all! Maybe our chance will come at another time. I say 'maybe' because I really don't believe any longer in a serious battle with England on English soil.**

I still don't know whether I'll be going to the military school on the 15th of January. To be honest with you, I'd rather stay here with my comrades and my company. The entire matter is still unresolved. There are twenty-three officer candidates left in our group here and it looks like this number will remain the same.

Well, what's new? I believe that you're right when you say that you have no intention of going home on your furlough. I simply don't understand Mother! She is incorrigible! By the way, since you sent Mother a fur coat, my little wife has also expressed an interest in owning one of these coats! You know how women are! Were you able to get some leather boots for her? Please write me soon and try to understand me.

Your loyal son, Karl

In this long letter to his father, Karl once again wonders why he isn't getting promoted and why he hasn't received his furlough. It is difficult to determine whether Karl felt that he deserved more attention because, in his opinion, he did more for the company than others or whether the system simply overlooked him.

*Hitler's plan to Germanize parts of western Poland, now incorporated into the Reich, involved forcible eviction of the ethnic Polish population and its replacement by Germans from almost everywhere in eastern Europe. It also involved "reconverting" those people of avowed German descent whose racial identity had been "submerged" in the Polish state. Village schoolmasters were to play an important role in this process, as living symbols of the New Order. A man like Karl was a logical candidate for the program: young, personable, idealistic—and bored with his current assignment.

**Karl's division was transferred from the Paris region south to Bordeaux in mid-November.

*   *   *   *   *

1 December 1940

Dearest Darling,

It's Sunday and the first of December. The sun is shining, the sky is blue, the air is fresh and we're listening to the hit parade on the radio. Everyone seems happy but I'm very sad. Again no letter from you. However, there was a letter from Father and it's a disturbing one. Please don't say anything about this to Mother. Apparently Father had a terrible accident and is in the hospital. His car was hit by a truck and both of his knees and legs are in bad shape. As you can imagine, I'm very upset about this. He wrote and said that he wouldn't tell Mother anything about it and so I beg you to respect his wishes. You know my Father and how he won't take this lying down. He thinks that it'll work out all right and that he'll be able to walk again. I just wish that I could go and see him, but these stupid NCO training courses do not permit any absences.

It was a year ago today that I was assigned to the tank corps and I really don't know what has happened to all that time. Soon the final battle will be fought and I'll come home to you without ever having been at the front. A moment ago Dr. Goebbels spoke on the radio and I hope that you were able to hear his words too. He spoke about German women and mothers who, at a great historical time like this one, are able to give birth to our children. You carry a young life in you now and must be very happy and proud. Certainly I'm proud of you and thank you again and again for your love. What are you doing right now? I often think of you and wish that my thoughts could fly to you like the music on the radio that comes to me from home. Do you often think of me, your little soldier? Do you long for me the way I long for you? I kiss and hug you.

Korri

*   *   *   *   *

8 December 1940

Dear Father,

What in the world are you doing? You shouldn't have let a huge truck crash into your little car! You certainly scared me with that bit of news, but I hope that you are not seriously hurt. I guess luck was on your side and the accident could have been much worse. You and I seem to be having quite a bit of luck these days. A week from tomorrow, on the 16th of December, I'm going to visit you. I discussed the matter with my First Sergeant today and he promised to get me a brief leave of absence.

Two days ago I almost had an accident as well, but it seems that the gods were with me, as I'm not yet on the casualty list. You know I'm responsible for next Sunday's Christmas festivities at company headquarters. I'm in charge of the musical presentations, both choral and instrumental. (On top of everything else, I'm getting in good with the First Sergeant and the C.O.)

Well, after last week's rehearsal, I drove home on a motorbike. I was going along at a pretty good clip when all of a sudden one of those two-wheeled carts which these French farmers use appeared in front of me. Naturally, these damn French farmers don't bother with reflectors or lights. At the last possible moment, I instinctively yanked the bike to the left and buzzed passed the cart at about 50 km an hour, just missing a steamroller that was parked on the side of the road! Well, as I said before, you've got to have luck!

I've got to sign off. I truly hope that everything will work out with our planned furlough. Until I see you, good-bye and a speedy recovery! Cheers!

Your loyal son, Karl

*   *   *   *   *

18 December 1940

Dearest Darling,

Today a restless vagabond is writing to you. Yes, we've really become gypsies in the last couple of days. We've had some maneuvers in the south of France and they took place in incredible conditions.* Sure, there are palm trees here but it's so dirty everywhere and the peasant huts look like cow sheds. I just have enough time to write you a few lines to let you know that I'm well, because the mail pick-up is at 7 o'clock. It's bad enough that the countryside is so desolate and depressing, but even more discouraging is an order that was just read a few moments ago: All leaves have been cancelled until December 21! You know very well what that means and you understand my disappointment. It looks like I won't be home for Christmas after all. Our only consolation is that thousands of men and women are suffering a similar fate. All my comrades and I have grown accustomed to living with disappointment; slowly but surely this is getting to be too much. I suppose the main thing is that all the bigwigs are home at Christmas. No need for the common soldier to go home!! It seems that no one worries about our emotional stability. You must understand that I'm slowly becoming angry about this whole mess. There still seems to be a ray of hope that I'll get a Christmas furlough, but it's not up to us.** Don't be sad and don't cry. I love you very much and forever.

Your Korri

*Though not specifically earmarked for Operation Felix, the proposed attack on Gibraltar, the 7th Panzer Division was part of the forces available to support Hitler's diplomatic pressure on Francisco Franco of this period. (Cf. Charles Burdick, *German Military Strategy and Spain in World War II* (Syracuse, N.Y., 1968).)

**Father and son did, in fact, receive parallel furloughs and were home for New Year's.

*   *   *   *   *

17 January 1941

Dearest Darling,

For the first time in a long time I got in late tonight. It's almost midnight. Yesterday morning at 6 a.m. we were ordered to report to a gunnery range in the vicinity of a large river delta. On the way we drove past some dilapidated buildings. It almost seemed like we were in Morocco with most of the people around us looking like bandits and gypsies. They appear so cunning and deceitful and some of them even hid on a little ridge and watched us train.

Now I'm extremely cold and dog-tired. It's very cold here. My lips and face are so dry that my skin has cracked. But I don't mind that.

You know by now that I'm a sergeant and have been promoted to train new recruits. This is, of course, a better position than being a mere corporal. I was even introduced to the Commander of the regiment the other day.*

Tomorrow is Saturday and then I'll have more time to write to you. Good night and lots of love,

Your Korri

P.S. By the way, I've talked to a number of other officer candidates and we all seem to be in agreement that it's best not to become career officers. I wouldn't want to be tied down for such a long time.

*Colonel Rothenburg had led the 25th Panzer Regiment through France, earning repeated praise for his aggressiveness and his tactical skills. He was equally proficient as a trainer.

* * * * *

20 January 1941

Dear Father,

By now you will be back at your old job. I hope that the last days of your furlough were restful and happy. How are things with our new apartment? I hope that Mother discussed the matter once more with Mrs. Winkler.

At the moment I'm in charge of instructing new recruits here, a job that I like very much. Being a sergeant is very different from being a corporal. Every Friday, however, I'm still with the regiment for officer candidate training. All of us here in the officer training program are still hoping to be sent to the front soon in order to participate in the final battle. We will make certain that our tank unit will do an honorable job.

This noon we had an important visitor, *Gauleiter* Sauckel from the District of Thuringia, who spoke to our company.* A tremendous fellow! At the end of the presentation, he gave us 250 RM to have a good time, at least that's what he said. Naturally, we will comply with his request! Otherwise nothing is new here.

At the end of my short letter, let me wish you a happy birthday. I hope that this coming year will bring us victory and peace. Sieg Heil!

Your loyal son, Karl

*Sauckel's presence can be explained by his status as *Gauleiter* of Thuringia, the 7th Panzer Division's recruiting area.

*   *   *   *   *

7 February 1941

Dear Father,

Thanks for your brief note. I'm glad that I remembered your birthday and that you received my greetings in time. It's too bad that you didn't receive any birthday greetings from anyone else in the family but I'm sure they'll be forthcoming.

All memories of my last furlough have vanished and the daily routine has moved into the foreground again. I'm really happy that the inspection of my recruits is over. It's not easy to conduct training that brings out the military potential in these young men since they are so naive and know nothing. But the training is hard and I believe the men appreciate that. This hard training is necessary when you consider what might be coming in the next weeks and months.* It's about time that we in the tank corps can prove that we're still around and that we can support our comrades of the Air Force and the Navy.

There's only one thing that I abhor and that's this eternal schooling for officer candidates. On April 1st they want me to go to a branch school.** That's exactly the time, however, when my comrades and my company will probably be engaged in battle. No, this time I want to participate fully and I'd rather forget being an officer. It seems to me that they could promote me to officer after I have proven myself in battle. They do that in other branches of the military. Why can't they do it in the tank corps? Never will I choose more training over a chance to fight!

It looks like we might be driving by your area during the next couple of days since our entire unit is scheduled to go back to Germany. Write me soon. I remain

your loyal son, Karl

*Karl's letters frequently indicate the emphasis Rommel and his regimental commanders placed on small-unit training. His new assignment as a recruit instructor reflected the doubling of the number of Panzer divisions in 1940–1941—a decision making corresponding demands on existing formations for cadres and specialists, and opening slots for new men.

**School for advanced training in armored warfare.

*   *   *   *   *

Nuremberg

27 February 1941

Dear Father,

Yesterday I arrived in Nuremberg and am happy to report that I have a week of furlough. Our unit was transferred from France to the Rhine River, a move which you, no doubt, anticipated.* In your last letter you wrote about possible military action in the spring. It really sounds strange now, particularly since your comments agree with the last speech of the Führer. I almost believe that I'll be able to stay here for at least three weeks and will be able to train here because headquarters seems to anticipate a major offensive soon. Well, we are as ready as you are.

Here in Germany my superiors have once more given me a choice—either assignment to the reserve battalion and branch school, or a call to the front in the near future. They really wanted to force me to go to branch school but I remained adamant and said no. I'm sick and tired of these idiotic courses. I'm convinced that we are stuck with these dumb courses because our commander loves to hear himself talk and loves to teach classes. But we've had it! I want to be part of the action! I want to prove that I'm a man! I don't want to be an officer unless I can become one by being at the front. I believe that you understand how I feel.

I can't speak this way to Mädi and to Mother because they would rather see me safe at home than at the front. But in the final analysis, this has to be the correct choice for me. Besides everything else, I've become such an integral part of my company that I couldn't leave it ever again. Furthermore, my superiors seem to like me. Just listen to this! A few days ago I was supposed to be transferred to another company, but this time my commander intervened in my behalf and the transfer was cancelled!

Well, now you know what's been happening around here lately. I'm very impressed to hear that you spoke with Franz Lehar. That's really exciting! Hearty greetings and Sieg Heil!

Your loyal son, Karl

*In February, the 7th Panzer Division was transferred to the Bonn-Bad Godesberg area for training and as a preliminary to its move farther eastward.

* * * * *

*Eschenau, on vacation**

11 March 1941

Dear Father,

. . . I'm scheduled to return to my unit in a week and my fervent wish is to participate in battle. Even though you may disagree with me about my plans, I want to ask you to put yourself in my shoes. Don't you think it's about time that the younger generation is given a chance? I mean, your son would also like to prove himself. You guys have achieved enough already. You've got a whole chestful of medals and stripes!

Fritz Bayn came through Rosstal with his unit a few days ago. Naturally his father and mother are very proud of him. Fritz, a couple of other guys and I spent half of Saturday night playing cards at the Eckert Inn. At least I've had lots of experience playing cards so I really skunked Willi and Geissler in the course of the evening. Nevertheless, they were nice to me and paid the entire bill. They're super guys! Hilde Bayn, by the way, is expecting a visit from the stork in early April. Isn't it amazing how blessed our Fatherland is with children? Certainly we don't have to worry about the future.

My young wife wrote to you yesterday. I don't know what to

say but I think that the two of you must have some secrets. She was smiling in a mysterious way when she put the letter into the envelope. She wouldn't even let me sign the letter. Mother and I are getting along famously. She is very nice to Mädi and me. At least we won't have to worry about our relationship when I have to leave again. On Sunday Mädi, Mother, the in-laws and I went to the Apollo Theater.** Great program!

Thank you for your birthday wishes and your promised present. You know what my wish is, namely, that I'll be called to the front and that I'll be proud of it. I wish you much luck as an Air Force officer. Good-bye and Auf Wiedersehen after the final battle.

Your loyal son, Karl

*This was Karl's last visit home before he was killed in action eight months later. He saw his wife only one more time, in April when she, seven months pregnant, came to his training site in the Rhineland.

**The Apollo, one of Nuremberg's most popular variety theaters, had been a favorite target of Nazi attacks before 1933 because of its allegedly risque, "anti-national" programs. Presumably this had changed under the Third Reich.

*   *   *   *   *

Near Bonn, in the Rhineland

23 March 1941

Dearest Darling,

Today was Armed Forces Day. The weather, however, didn't cooperate. It rained the entire night and when I went to work, at 6:30 a.m., it wasn't much better. Two hours later it began to snow. You can imagine how we looked during the parade, soaked to the skin. But that really can't bother us soldiers. Our eyes and faces were aglow with the joy of triumph. We had reason for celebrating because twice our company was victorious in athletic competition. You should've seen your husband run in the 400m relays! Yup, I've still got it! I think I'm faster now than I ever was. Once the athletic competition was over, the musical competition started. We came out on top here as well. I was really proud of the choral group because it was basically due to my efforts that the group performed so well. The company commander personally congratulated me and spoke highly of my abilities. You know, if you were congratulated like this for every achievement, life would be much more pleasant. In most instances, though, it's just a matter of doing your duty. In recognition of our talents, our company received 200 RM for these victories. In a couple of hours I have to be ready to play the piano for my comrades. You know that I like to do that because, for the most part, they are all great guys. . . .

Love, Korri

P.S. Tomorrow I have to go to the dentist. I've got a bad toothache. It must be some kind of an infection, but I hope it'll feel better soon.

*   *   *   *   *

25 March 1941

Dearest Darling,

I have to go to the dentist again today. He was a bit rough in his treatment but I guess he couldn't help it. I've really been in pain. No wonder; the infection had progressed to a serious state and had begun to fester. Now I'm not permitted to smoke but maybe that's a good thing because I want to cut down anyway. You know I really would like to take part in more athletic activity and stay fit. That is why I want to cut down on my smoking. I don't think I can give it up completely, but I'll try. I know that this decision will make you happy, right? . . .

Yugoslavia joined the Axis powers today and that brought us quite a bit closer to victory and peace.* Yes, we really believed the words of the Führer now when he said that England would surely fall this year. Once that victory is accomplished and once I am honorably discharged, then I will come to you. We'll go into our child's room where, in a little crib, our baby will be sleeping. Then I'll take you by the hand very slowly and embrace you. I will kiss your white forehead to thank you for everything and to let you know that I will adore and love you for my entire life.

Yours in love, Korri

P.S. Thanks for all the books you have sent me. So far I have read four novels by Schroer; *Sturm im Sichdichtur, Der Heiland vom Binsenhof, Der rechte Erbe* and *Um Mannes Ehre.*** Please send me a couple of other books. Thanks.

*Yugoslavia's adherence to the Tripartite Pact was extremely brief. On 27 March an anti-Axis coup brought a military government to power and triggered Hitler's Balkan offensive. (Cf. Martin van Creveld, *Hitler's Strategy, 1940–1941: The Balkan Clue* (Cambridge, 1984).)

**Gustav Schroer (1876–1949) was a writer of novels dealing with traditional peasant and small-town life in Germany. The popularity of his works antedated but did not survive the Third Reich.

*　*　*　*　*

27 March 1941

Dear Mother,

Many thanks for your recent letter. Yes, I too think often and fondly of the weeks that we spent together. But let's not think about the past; let's think about the future and believe in it. Since Yugoslavia has joined the Axis powers, we are closer to victory and peace than ever before. We can now believe that the war will be over this year. We can trust our Führer completely. You know that as well as I do. So let's gladly make our small sacrifices now since they are made to give our children and grandchildren a better life. Yes, they will live in peace and harmony in the great Fatherland. For that goal, no sacrifice is too great. . . .

Our military activity is intermittent at best. Last night the Tommies visited us again, but it's never as bad as it sounds. Apparently they are running out of strength and fly over us only with weakened forces. Once we spot them with our searchlights, they disappear quickly into the concentrated fire of our antiaircraft guns. They have no courage.*

So here we sit and wait for things to happen. Hearty greetings and I wish you good health.

Your loyal son, Korri

P.S. Is our apartment at the Winkler's confirmed?

*Through the winter of 1940–1941, the RAF continued to mount small-scale, ineffective night raids over western Germany. Karl's evaluation of their limited, nuisance value is confirmed in Anthony Verrier, *The Bomber Offensive* (New York, 1968).

*   *   *   *   *

1 April 1941

My dearest wife,

I received another letter from you today. Every time one of your letters arrives, I am so unbelievably happy! Mädi, you must be particularly careful now being seven months pregnant. You know what I mean. Tomorrow I'll write to you and tell you when I will call you on the telephone. I'm still checking on the possibilities of the two of us getting together. I won't make any hasty decisions, you know that. Normally when I make a decision, I do the right thing, except when it comes to taking pictures! You know I can't do that very well because it seems that every time I take a picture of you, you end up in the corner of the photo. I'm really sorry that I missed your head, but everything else is there!

This coming Sunday three friends of mine and I are going to Cologne to watch the international soccer game between Germany and Hungary.* I'm really looking forward to this game since I have a keen interest in soccer, as you well know. We have excellent seats, but they did cost 5 RM per person.

This evening all of us NCO's are having another party. These parties never seem to end! Well, we still have champagne from France and the idea is to drink it up this evening. Why not? In a few days all these festivities will be over anyway. You can imagine how mad all of us are about the actions of these Goddamn Yugoslavs.** There is simply no telling what they will do next. But we'll teach them a lesson yet, those gypsies with their King Peter II.

I'm looking forward to the huge package which you promised to send me.

Love and kisses, Your Korri

*This was not a cup match, but a *Freundschaftsspiel*. The decision to hold the game under wartime conditions and with wartime risks indicates the Nazi regime's concern to maintain as many of the elements of "normal" civilian life as possible. Hitler was unwilling to put any more strain on public morale than seemed absolutely necessary. He believed firmly that Germany's defeat in 1918 was caused by the home front's collapse and he did not wish to risk a repetition. Germany, in passing, defeated Hungary 7–0.

**Their three-day flirt with the Axis powers had ended abruptly.

* * * * *

Along the Rhine

7 April 1941

My dear Darling,

Yesterday I attended the international soccer game in Cologne. It was a fabulous match! Unfortunately the weather was bad; first it snowed and then it rained. The weather here, at least for the time being, is miserable. Did you receive my picture postcard from Cologne? Naturally, you know this city a lot better than I do since you are from the Rhineland and I'm only a common Bavarian! I'm only joking!

Aside from this spectacular soccer battle, there happens to be another battle raging. We all expected this battle which started several hours ago. We are confident that our German soldiers will teach those Yugoslav bums a lesson once and for all. How dare they point the dagger at us? And what are we doing here? We are sitting around like always and are waiting for our call to the front.

Yesterday I received two letters from you, one sweeter than the other. In one you wrote how much you can feel our baby move. I think that maybe that ten-hour train trip from Nuremberg to here will be too much of a strain on you. I talked with Mr. Friedrichs* today. He had just received two days vacation and he thought that it was very irresponsible for me to encourage you to take this long trip.

Well, it's 2 a.m. again and I need some sleep. No action from the Tommies tonight. I only wish that we could get to those damn English dogs! It's high time that this battle for England began anew. I have a strange feeling that pretty soon we'll see some action. We all think, though, that Yugoslavia is the likely spot. Well, no matter what the future brings, we'll be ready and will fight for our loved ones at home. I love you dearly and want to give you and our unborn baby a big hug.

Your Korri

*The family with which Karl was billeted. Mrs. Friedrichs, pregnant at the time, agreed to accept Karl only after the billeting officer had spoken of Karl as the "Professor." She has fond memories of Karl, and kept as mementoes several letters which he wrote to her from the Russian front.

*   *   *   *   *

9 April 1941

Dear Father,

Our Führer has once again called upon his soldiers and once more they are all marching, this time against Yugoslavia and Greece. We, however, are situated somewhere in Germany and have to watch how our comrades reap victory upon victory. I guess I haven't had one iota of luck, as far as becoming a front soldier is concerned. But I keep on hoping and I know that sooner or later it will be my turn and it may be somewhere in the East. What do you think? All day long we have been hearing special announcements on the radio such as "Soloniki captured!" and "Penetration to the Aegean Sea!" or "The Greek East Army has capitulated!"* All these announcements cause our hearts to beat quicker and our thoughts are with our comrades. It certainly is something wonderful and special, that German soldier spirit. I guess the English can only be astonished by this and just watch.

. . . Easter is just around the corner and my wife wants to visit me for a couple of days. In her present condition, though, I don't know if that would be wise—I mean, the baby is to be born in seven weeks. Ten hours on the train is probably not the best thing for her right now. But if she wants to come, I can't change her mind.

Mother sent me a little package for Easter with cookies and cigarettes. I especially liked the cigarettes because they seem to have become a rare commodity. Let's hope that sooner or later the hour of my active participation in the war will arrive. Happy Easter and lots of luck.

Your son, Karl

*Several Panzer divisions had spearheaded the *Wehrmacht*'s drive through the Balkans.

*   *   *   *   *

17 April 1941

Dear Mädi,

I received your postcard today which informed me that you arrived home in good shape. I was happy to hear that. If you had stayed a few more days, it wouldn't have been worth it because at the moment we're working from 6 a.m. until 8 p.m. Even at night we don't have any peace and quiet. I wrote to you about the air-raid drill and the best thing about it was that it didn't work at all. Now our superiors have sworn that we have to repeat the drill again and again until they are satisfied that it works! That's no skin off our backs. Looks like they are going to boot us out of our bunks again this evening, but who cares! The important thing is that keg of beer which you had bought has been emptied. Twelve of us finished it off Tuesday evening and everyone drank enthusiastically. One of the boys climbed up on top of the keg and gave a speech. It was his opinion that all German women should be like you, my dear, because at least you took care of the thirst of the German noncommissioned officers! It was really a very nice speech and we all enjoyed ourselves.

Here is something that you won't believe! Yesterday I went to church! Yes, one of our NCO's got married and after the civil ceremony, we all went to church. First, I was asked to give a little speech in his behalf and since the church had no organist, I sat down at the organ and played some appropriate music. Thus, I was able to provide a bit of joy for a good comrade and his young wife. During the entire ceremony I had to think of our own wedding. In a few days we could celebrate our first anniversary if we were together.

I love you very much.

Your Korri

*   *   *   *   *

25 April 1941

My dearest Darling,

A year ago today we were married! I can hardly believe how quickly the time has gone by. But let's not think of the year that has passed and the few times that we were together; let's think of the future, believe in it and hope that the second year of our marriage will be spent together.

Do you know what song I played on the piano today? "Majarska!" I was all alone in the house here; even old Mrs. Friedrichs was gone. Outside the trees were bending in the wind and the white blossoms on the linden trees smelled so fresh and so I began to play and sing. There wasn't a picture of you in the room but, nevertheless, you appeared before me. I saw you and all your lovely features quite clearly. I felt the closeness of you and sensed how strong and eternal my love is for you. I was truly happy.

I must tell you that Father has had another accident! This news was disconcerting but thank God it isn't too serious. He'll need medical care for two weeks or so. I'll write him immediately, of course. Mother seems to be sick again. I really want to thank you for taking care of her and I'll also write her a letter this evening.

All of us here in the unit have been inoculated and the right side of my chest is swollen so that I can hardly raise my arm. On top of that, I have a fever; one minute I'm freezing and the next I'm sweating. Well, this too will pass.

On our wedding anniversary, I embrace you and kiss you tenderly.

Your Korri

*   *   *   *   *

28 April 1941

My dearest Mädi,

This evening we returned from maneuvers, frozen stiff!* We were in the Ahr Valley of the Eifel Mountains. Back there, spring has not progressed as quickly as you might expect. Not a tree or a bush is yet in bloom. As a matter of fact, it still looks like it's winter and on Monday it snowed there. Otherwise, this rough region is quite beautiful, at least as far as the landscape is concerned. While traveling there I often thought of how nice it would be if you and I could go walking hand-in-hand through the valleys. You need to visualize a very narrow valley, with exposed cliffs on both sides. In the middle of the valley, there is a little carpet of a meadow with a happily meandering brook. Oh Mädi, I long for you frequently and would like to be with you. I want to love you and yet I'm not permitted to visit you. I shouldn't even speak about it because I know that this longing must hurt you. But your feelings must be the same. They are documented in all the letters that I receive from you. You can't imagine how happy I am when I read the letters.

Let's think of the times when we will be together for always. I want so much to put my head against your cheeks and kiss you.

Your Korri

*Karl was serving under a new commanding general. Rommel had been transferred on 14 February. His successor, General Freiherr von Funck, was to prove a worthy replacement and an equally hard driver.

*   *   *   *   *

29 April 1941

Dear Father,

I have finally received a letter from you. Mädi had already written to me about your accident and now I am getting the details in your letter. I must say that you're certainly fortunate to be all right but you seem to be having an unlucky streak as far as accidents are concerned. I want to wish you a speedy recovery.

Yes, my dear Father, you should have pity on me! Have you ever known a person who always comes too late and who can only admire the glorious deeds of others? This is a deplorable situation for me! While you fly against the Tommies and while other comrades of mine are able to prove their courage again and again, I have to stand here at some home base, forever ready, going to one maneuver after another and polishing my tank day-in and day-out. All for what? I don't even remember how many times I've been inoculated and x-rayed, or how many medical examinations I've had! It certainly looks like the war will be over before they see fit to send me to the front. If I had known that, I would have volunteered for the Air Force right away. Yes, if, if, if—damn it all! Maybe there's still a chance for me.*

This afternoon we had an air raid. It was the first time that the air raid was called during the day, but nothing came of it. I guess the Tommies must have chickened out.

Well, dear Father, I greet you with our old battle cry, "Germany, Sieg Heil!"

Your loyal son, Karl

*These emotions, common enough to men at war, seem to have been particularly strong in the German armored and motorized divisions in the spring of 1941. They had seen just enough combat to find the thought of another challenge stimulating; they thought themselves too much the old soldiers to endure patiently training routines that seemed direct carryovers from peacetime. This sequence of letters also reinforces another point frequently overlooked in the academic literature. The German *Landser* of World War II was, at least at this stage, not a universal soldier waging a forever war. He wanted above all to go home, and was constantly buoyed by hopes that peace was just beyond the next victory.

*   *   *   *   *

6 May 1941

My dearest Darling,

It's 11 p.m. and I just returned from a twelve-hour training mission. Just to show you how nice our superiors are to us, we've been instructed to get up at 4:30 a.m. to work double shifts during the day. Yes, in the last couple of weeks, it's been like this every day. We have practically no free time.

This morning I received two letters, one from you and the other from Mother. Both are full of complaints. They are not very edifying and neither of them does much to lift my spirits. I too have contemplated this apartment matter time and time again, but I simply can't find a solution. The two of us just don't have an apartment! . . . Couldn't you find a furnished room somewhere? This situation is really getting me down. Sometimes I shake my head in disgust when I think of what our government demands of its people—to marry young, have children and then to discover that there are no apartments for them to live in!* I think and worry about you continually and it makes me feel terrible to know that you are all on your own. If Father were only at home to help out! I'm sure that he would find a solution to this perplexing situation. His condition, however, has worsened and he can't travel. It seems that in our family, misfortune strikes several blows all at once; Mother is sick, Father is in the military hospital and you are emotionally upset. I'm reeling, totally helpless and confused. Perhaps it's because I'm so damn tired.

My thoughts are with you and I worry about you and our unborn child.

Your Korri

*Germany's general housing shortage, chronic since the Empire, had been exacerbated by massive wartime dislocations. A young married couple seeking even a furnished room needed family or political connections on the spot—something Karl and Mädi lacked.

*   *   *   *   *

13 May 1941

Dearest Mädi,

Last night we had another air raid for a change. It was nothing to worry about. The only thing was that it ruined a couple hours of sleep! But we're used to that by now.

Last night we were shocked when we heard of the mysterious fate of Rudolf Hess. Today's news seems to explain the whole affair. Nevertheless, the circumstances surrounding this flight certainly seem weird.*

I was daydreaming today and it seemed that I heard church bells toll, announcing peace. But for the time being, that's a mere *fata morgana*. One day peace will come and your tired soldier will come home and rest his head in your lap. In the early morning hours, in spite of the air raid, I still had a dream of you and our child. The child was lovely and had a blue blanket wrapped around him, the blanket I sent you from France. When I go to sleep tonight, I'll wish for another beautiful dream just like this one. I love you so very much.

Your Korri

P.S. Included is my military pay statement. Don't lose it. Joseph wrote to me today. Yes, he was where the action is, in the Balkans and even in Athens. I still haven't seen any action. He gave me his new address. Make a note of it for the birth announcements.

*On 12 May 1941 Hitler's deputy führer, Rudolf Hess, flew a Messer-schmitt 110 to England where he proclaimed a one-man effort to negoti-ate a peace settlement. Hitler promptly declared that Hess had lost his mind. Hess, sentenced to life imprisonment for war crimes, remains incarcerated in Spandau Prison as of this writing.

* * * * *

17 May 1941

Dear Darling,

It's Saturday and I'm off-duty today. For these few hours today and tomorrow I'll spend hiking in the surrounding hills. But now I'm in my room, sitting next to a huge bunch of blooming elderberries. I'm also listening to some magnificent "music." This "music" is not coming from the radio but out of the mouth of little Inge! Yes sir, if our child screams as much as she does, we'll have our hands full! I really don't mind the screaming too much. I've even rocked the baby a couple of times and have sung her to sleep. I'm practicing for my upcoming fatherhood!

This evening the Royal Air Force visited us again. These Tommies are just a bunch of dirty dogs! According to the official army report, they threw their incendiary bombs aimlessly over the countryside. It must have been a stroke of good luck that this time no civilians were killed. Apparently these pigs have assumed a new tactic, namely, to intimidate the public with their bomb-ings. This plan certainly won't work with our people.*

No letter from you today and I was sad. I'll have to console myself and look forward to tomorrow's letter since tomorrow is Mother's Day. Just think, Mädi, soon you'll be a mother too and can be happy with our child. Then the two of you will wait for the day when I come home. Love and kisses.

Yours for always, Korri

*Karl was anticipating events here. Systematic area attacks did not begin until 1942. At this stage, inexperience, fatigue, and technical shortcomings had much more to do with the scattershot bombing pat-terns Karl frequently describes.

* * * * *

20 May 1941

My dearest Darling,

Today was a very sad day for me and the rest of my comrades. We carried a fellow officer to his grave, an officer who was one of the best and who was accidentally killed while on duty. Particularly touching was the scene when his wife and their two children stood in front of the coffin. Yes, that's the way life is. It's over very quickly. But we want to live; we want to live on because life for us is just beginning. We really have not yet had much of life and want the chance to experience a lot together. Once this war is over, once there's an end to all this madness, I want to work for you and our child. I want to create a happy and carefree life for us. I believe that fate has given me this task and I know that I will come back to you. My dearest, don't fear for me. I will return. I love both of you.

Your Korri

*   *   *   *   *

23 May 1941

My dearest Mädi,

. . . I want to tell you about the film I saw last night.* It was called "Willy Birgel Rides for Germany." What a magnificent performance by this star! I was also impressed by the plot, especially at the end of the film. In order to understand the film, you have to recollect the time when a German officer had to defend the honor of his Fatherland against a world of enemies. Here this honor was defended in a riding contest in which he, the German officer, finally was victorious. The final scenes were not only touching but also uplifting. Three German people stand there at the grand finale of the film: first, like a bronze statue, a victorious rider and his horse; then a little German girl joins them. At this point the former second lieutenant from the Great War breaks into tears upon hearing our national anthem. Yes, it was a very moving final scene.

At the beginning of this letter, I told you that I felt your protective presence today. Now after you read the next lines, please don't get upset. My friend Roland picked me up this evening to go to the movies and we drove to town on his motorcycle. While driving, he skidded on the wet street and slid into a house with the bike. Nothing happened to me at all—just a few bruises and a minor contusion. It's midnight and I'm home now. Roland, however, wasn't so lucky and is in the hospital. He suffered a few cuts and lacerations and had to get stitches. Yes, my dear, I'm quite well and healthy and know that I will live long for you and our child.

Your Korri

*Karl had seen an early showing of *Willy Birgel reitet für Deutschland,* released in April 1941. It was the kind of film he was likely to enjoy: fast-paced and permeated with nationalist and soldierly values. (Cf. David Stewart Hull, *Film in the Third Reich,* reprint ed. (New York, 1973), 195.)

* * * * *

24 May 1941

My darling Mädi,

I'm sorry to report to you that your husband is presently limping, but in a couple of days I guess my leg will feel much better. It was just a little motorcycle accident and the wounds are superficial. I certainly learned something from this accident: luck seems to be on my side and you, my darling, protect this luck with your love.

. . . In your recent letter you tell me of a dream, a dream in which I have been assigned to an eight-week course in Erlangen, close to home. Yes, my dear, that would be beautiful and we could be happy with our baby, but you must realize that you have to be courageous. Believe me, this courage will be rewarded one of these days. I know that for certain. During wartime a woman has only one soul and this soul fears for the life of her husband—that's all. A man, however, has two souls in difficult times—indeed, he must have two: The one soul expresses the sincere wish to be home with his beloved; the other soul wants to be engaged in battle and to be victorious. This feeling for battle and victory must be the more important one in a man, because this struggle is not only for his loved ones in particular but also for his

Fatherland in general. You see, my dear, I understand you like no one else. Your longing, love and care for me make me proud, but you too have to understand me. Life, by definition, means struggle and he who avoids this struggle or fears it is a despicable coward and does not deserve to live.* You need not worry about me. Be courageous!! I love you forever.

Korri

*This sentiment, while paralleling many in *Mein Kampf* and equivalent Nazi propaganda, also shows the strong influence of vulgarized Social Darwinism on German intellectual life. In this, as in so many other ways, National Socialism was a magpie movement, picking up, repeating, and magnifying ideas already existing rather than introducing entirely new themes and concepts. (For a useful survey, see Hans-Gunter Zmarzlik, "Social Darwinism in Germany, seen as a Historical Problem," in *Republic to Reich: The Making of the Nazi Revolution,* ed. Hugo Hollan (New York, 1972), 435–74.)

*　*　*　*　*

25 May 1941

Dearest Mädi,

Another Sunday. There's light rain and a breeze coming from the West. I'm sitting here, counting and thinking of what will happen in about fourteen days. Yes, in about two weeks our happiest day and our proudest hour will arrive. I can hardly wait any longer! I'm pleased to hear that you've prepared the little room upstairs. Yes, I too would like so much to see how you've fixed it up. I know that everything you've done for the baby has been done with loving care.

And what do you think of yesterday? It certainly was an eventful day for Germany. German paratroopers landed on the island of Crete!* There was also a sea battle off the coast of Iceland and we sank one of the biggest battleships in the world.** Splendid —indeed, splendid! That, my dear, is German military spirit. Can you understand that all of us here sit around with tears in our eyes because we have to watch these heroic deeds from afar! We're sitting here in the Fatherland and feel like incompetent idiots!

The telephone just rang and everytime it does, I think it'll be you with the happiest news of all! You just can't imagine how I'm looking forward to the day when our child will be born. I agree with you about the names, Horst Harro for the boy or Karin for the girl. These names are fine with me.

And you're still going to the theatre! I can hardly believe it but I do know how much you love Franz Lehar's melodies! When I return, I'll play all these melodies for you and will sing them with my best voice. I want to hug and kiss you.

Love, Korri

*The airborne assault on Crete actually began on 20 May. Karl's enthusiasm was influenced by propaganda broadcasts based on exaggerated pilots' reports. The Royal Navy, though badly hammered by air attacks, lost no warship larger than a cruiser.

**The H.M.S. *Hood* was sunk off Iceland by the *Bismarck* on 24 May 1941.

*   *   *   *   *

27 May 1941

My little Sweetheart and dearest Darling,

We just heard on the radio about our poor, brave comrades on the Battleship *Bismarck*.* We're very moved by the unfortunate situation and the fate which has befallen these men at sea. They fought and died for us but live on in us. Isn't it strange how tragedies like this one bring people closer together? It's because we admire and pity these heroes. I'm sure that you back home in Nuremberg feel the same way. It's just so damn unfortunate and unfair that the best and bravest men always must die. We want to and will avenge the deaths of our comrades. We are certain of this. An individual is comparatively insignificant in war and yet, individual sacrifice in the struggle for an ideal is not in vain. Peace and victory will come from these sacrifices and today we believe, in spite of everything we've heard, that there'll be a speedy end to this war.

A few days ago I told you about the accident which Roland and I had. Today my superiors questioned me about this incident and my commander told me that I would probably get two or three weeks in the guardhouse because I didn't tell the driver, who is a lieutenant, to drive more slowly! Isn't that ridiculous? I can't understand this decision but I really don't give a damn! I only hope that my dear comrade Roland will recover completely. Unfortunately, the doctors feel that he will have a permanently stiff leg. The x-rays show that the knee joint of his right leg has been severely damaged. This afternoon I wanted to visit him but my duties here prevented me from going. I'm just terribly sorry for him and just can't imagine what he'll do if he, indeed, will end up with a stiff leg. And they want to arrest me! I just can't understand it. If that happens, of course, I won't be able to see you at all. It certainly wasn't my fault. Why should I, a sergeant, have to warn a lieutenant to drive more slowly?**

For you and the baby, I send my best wishes.

Love, Korri

*The *Bismarck's* Atlantic sortie, which began on 18 May, ended with her crippling by British torpedo planes and her destruction by gunfire and surface torpedoes on 26 and 27 May. (For the way Goebbels handled the event, see particularly Jay Baird, *The Mythical World of Nazi War Propaganda, 1938–1945* (Minneapolis, 1974), 142–43.) Here, as in his reaction to *Kristallnacht,* Karl was far less critical than many of his countrymen.

**"Because shit runs downhill in all armies" is the answer. Ultimately nothing came of the affair; the 25th Panzer Regiment had more to occupy its attention than a traffic accident.

*   *   *   *   *

30 May 1941

Dear Mother,

It took me a couple of days to get over your letter and I still can't comprehend it! I have given this letter much thought and contemplation. I am much calmer now and have come to the conclusion that what is at fault are the difficult times in which we live. I do think, though, that in times like these, people ought to grow more supportive of each other, be more tied to their children and become closer and should not quarrel. I would never have guessed that you judge my father-in-law Gustav the way you do. He never did you or Father any harm—just as you never harmed him. Do you know what the worst thing in the world is?

It's hatred. Hatred ruins entire peoples and certainly can ruin individuals as well. And here I sit, far away from home and I've got to read letters about all of these quarrels. It certainly is a depressing feeling for me. Unfortunately, I can't get away from here; otherwise, I'm certain that I could have smoothed over these quarrels.

I'm terribly disappointed that I won't be able to witness the birth of my first child. At that time, we shall no longer be stationed here. Believe me, those are real worries.

Well, Mädi is at home now in Nuremberg with her parents and that situation will also resolve itself. I don't want to judge you, but as a human being who is rational and has feelings, I would like to give you all a little bit of advice: Please try to get along with each other! This present situation is unbearable. Do you think that it's comforting to me so far away from home and about to enter battle to know that my loved ones at home are quarreling? Please consider this and act accordingly.

One thing I know for sure that will hold true as long as I live is that I honor you as my parents and I love you; but I will always support my wife and stand firmly behind her, no matter what happens.

I wish you a speedy recovery from your ill health and remain forever

your loyal son, Karl

*   *   *   *   *

1 June 1941

My dearest Sweetheart,

Today is Pentecost, the first of June. June is the month that will bring us our most beautiful present ever, our long-awaited beloved child. You, my darling, will have to endure quite a bit of pain in a few days. If I could only be with you!

Important, beautiful and holy things don't simply happen, you have to fight for them, fight for them with all your might! That makes you strong and sturdy and is the same for a man or a woman. There's simply no difference. The struggle for existence, whether we are talking about a man or a woman, creates proud, free, honest and upright people. All others will remain repulsive creeps, inferior individuals who shy away from danger and who, when the chips are down, will succumb to that danger. No matter what comes, I'll always face life with confidence and expectation. I know that I will be victorious.

I'm looking out of my window now and see that the sun has broken through the thick fog which hovered over the land. Isn't that a symbol of the strength of human beings? Now sunshine is everywhere and the blue of the sky is overwhelming. That's the way it is in nature and also with human beings.

Yesterday I had quite a bit to do but in the evening I had time to visit Roland in the hospital. He's feeling much better but he will have to be bedridden for at least another eight weeks. Poor fellow!

My thoughts are with you in your most difficult and happiest hours. I kiss you with all my love.

Your Korri

*   *   *   *   *

3 June 1941

My dearest Darling,

. . . I can understand your pain and sorrow because you have to be so alone now. Yet, I can't provide any comfort or any consolation; indeed, I must ask you to be strong and firm. Look, my dear, your husband today stands in the midst of a proud and difficult time. He is a soldier—not a civilian—and as a soldier he has duties to his Fatherland. These duties are important and sacred. You must learn today, even if it hurts, that your personal desires and wishes must be set aside. After all, we're not fighting just for you and me; we are fighting for the existence of our entire people, of our *Volk*. All of us who live in these times cannot permit ourselves to make the mistake of only thinking of ourselves. Our vision must be for the future because we are engaged in a struggle that will assure us of the well-being of our growing children and our nation. Please understand if I'm unable to write to you this week. . . .*

Love, Korri

*The 7th Panzer Division was at this time completing preparations to depart for the East. Its troop trains began leaving the Bonn region on 6 June.

*   *   *   *   *

On the move to the East

12 June 1941

Dearest Mädi,

By now our child has, no doubt, been born. If I only knew how you are feeling and whether it's a boy or a girl. I hope that everyone is kind and helpful to you now and that they are giving you some of the love that I would give you if I were there. Please write to me as soon as you can and tell me what the baby looks like. Once the two of you are out of the hospital, please send me a photo right away. I want to have the two of you close to me—as I will always belong to you.

The departure from our army base where we've been stationed so long was a real ceremony and very uplifting. We pulled out of there with our tanks decorated with flowers! The townspeople had given us many small presents and were very nice to us. That was several days ago, however, and now your big boy is sleeping on hay and straw. Since we are having such terrible weather all of a sudden—wind, rain and cold, I'm freezing! But since we're soldiers, that's not supposed to bother us.

Now we're sitting here—waiting. We don't know what our next orders will be. Whatever they are, don't fear for me. We're rather isolated from the world—no beer, no wine. Isn't it funny how life can change all of a sudden.

The other day I got a letter from the Superintendent of Schools in Weissenburg. He explained to me that he would like to consider me for a position in the secondary schools. Before we took off, I answered his letter and accepted his offer.* I'm sure that you will agree with me that this is a good position in as much as it is secondary school. This would also mean more pay. At any rate, we would live in a small city. The subjects that I chose were history, physical education and music. I know that you are in agreement with me. I'm with you in my thoughts. Stay healthy and strong. Lots of kisses to you both.

Your Korri

*Another indication of the belief, fairly widespread in Germany, that the war would come to a quick end after the stunning Axis victories in the Mediterranean. As a reserve officer candidate, Karl could expect reasonably quick demobilization. His optimism was, no doubt, also fostered by his strong desire to establish a home for his wife and new baby—and to reknit domestic relationships which he at least perceived as having been significantly frayed by the war. Weissenburg had the obvious advantage of being at a reasonable distance from parents and in-laws.

*   *   *   *   *

13 June 1941

My dearest Darling,

The happiest day of my life is today! I will always remember it! I'll remember the moment when I opened the telegram with trembling hands. My shining eyes displayed my happiness, my pride and my sincerest gratitude for what you have given me. I had to be alone for a while, alone with my thoughts and with you. Again and again I read the few words of the telegram. You have presented me with a boy! A strong baby boy! My darling Mädi, how shall I ever thank you?

When I am again in your arms and when I'm with you and our son, then we shall experience nothing but good fortune and sunshine. I'll come back to you; I know it for certain. Sooner or later I'll come home to you forever. Now you hold this sacred present in your arms, you, a young, proud German mother. When you look at the baby, when you caress him and feed him, you'll see in this boy a piece of my happiness. I know that you two are infinitely happy, just as I am, and we also know that this child will make our love grow and bring us closer together.

Next to me is your picture, the one you sent me not too long ago. My thoughts see you lying in a white bed with our lovely, young child slumbering peacefully next to you. Kiss the baby, caress him for me. You, my dear wife, may be assured of my everlasting love.

Yours forever, Korri

*   *   *   *   *

15 June 1941

Dear Father,

First of all, let me shake your hand and congratulate you for having become a grandfather! I know you'll understand that I'm overjoyed and proud. So you were right several months ago when you guessed that the baby would be a boy! That, in itself, is enough of a reason to celebrate, but unfortunately there is no way that I can do that here. We have neither wine nor beer and we're sitting here in the midst of nowhere! But be that as it may, it's more important for me to know that this child, this boy, will hopefully bring the members of the family back together again. It's sad, though, especially for my young wife, that I can't go home. The duty to the Fatherland is probably more important at this point and hopefully I'll be able to fulfill this duty soon in battle. I'm counting on it. For the time being, however, all of us in the unit are living quite a lonely existence, sleeping on hay.* It's somewhat romantic but it would be so much better if the weather were more cooperative. It's cold and rainy and on occasions the sun peeks through, but generally it's like April.

Today is Sunday and you won't believe it, but we played soccer for four hours straight. It really was fun, especially since we have a number of good players in our ranks.

I send my warmest greetings to you. I remain

your loyal son, Karl

*At this time the 7th Panzer Division was stationed southeast of Lötzen in East Prussia.

*   *   *   *   *

15 June 1941

Dear Mrs. Friedrichs,

I send you glad tidings of joy! My wife has presented me with a boy!! You can imagine that I'm so happy and proud that I don't know what to do. I know what you can do, though! Get little Inge ready for the young fox!! Maybe we'll be related in twenty years.

In my present loneliness I often think of those happy hours spent in your village of Rüdinghoven. Let me only remember the happy hours; let's forget all that gossip that was spread about me. I'm not interested in that anymore. My buddy Heyer told me that your mother-in-law shed a tear or two because I, the ungrateful person that I am, didn't stop by to thank her for the couple of cups of coffee I had at her place. Sorry about that, but it's water under the bridge now.

Too bad we don't sleep under those cozy red and white down comforters of yours anymore. Now straw and hay keep us warm. Pretty romantic, you might think, but not when you consider the nightly concerts orchestrated by a pack of rats. And I won't even mention the mosquito bites that cover my gorgeous body! "Gentlemen! And now a glass of punch!" Do you remember those bacchanalian pronouncements of yours? What nectar of the gods! And what quenches our thirst here? Sure, we have a couple of bottles of Rhine wine left, but that's it; there is no more!

You are probably glad to be rid of us, thinking that we will never change for the better. Don't worry, instead of engaging in drinking bouts we now compete in athletic contests. Four hours of soccer today, how about that? We have to toughen up our bodies and get ready for battle. Let's hope that our superiors don't test our patience again. We are ready.

I send you hearty greetings and thank you once more for everything.

Your Karl Fuchs

This is the first of ten letters which Karl wrote to Mrs. Friedrichs from the East. Karl had been billeted in her house during his training days in the Bonn area and had become a member of the family. Mrs. Friedrichs, who is still alive today, spoke affectionately of the "soldier boys" whose exploits she could remember vividly.

*　*　*　*　*

17 June 1941

Dearest Darling, my dear little Horsti,

Today I received your first letter after the birth of our son and I have to read it over and over because I am so extremely happy! At least now I can picture the little one and I'm able to see him right in front of me with his blue eyes, his stubby nose, and the pronounced indentation of his upper lip. I suppose it is only proper that he has inherited traits from both of us. Mädi, I know that our child is so sweet and one day he'll become a brave fellow, even though at birth he displayed two deep wrinkles on his little forehead. (You have these wrinkles, too, you know, but only when you're angry!) I'm looking forward to rearing and teaching our boy with you and am certain that our efforts will have positive results. . . .

Our status at present here at this temporary base is still uncertain. No one knows what is going to happen to us but we feel that some kind of decision will be forthcoming in a matter of days—if not in a matter of hours.* We all sense that something is about to happen. Don't worry about me. When I come home to you, my love for you will be much more mature since it has ripened in the experience and duration of this struggle. I'm calm, collected and at peace and look forward to the ensuing battle, because I know that I must live for you. I feel that you are with me and that you are protecting me. My deepest love for you and the baby.

Korri

*On 18 June elements of the 7th Panzer Division moved up the Russo-German border to secure assembly areas for the attack scheduled for 21 June.

* * * * *

The Eastern Front, Lithuania

25 June 1941

Dearly beloved Mädi,

Today was a day of pride for us all! Victoriously we marched into Vilnius [Lithuania], cheered on by the jubilant citizens. Yesterday I knocked off a Russian tank, as I had done two days ago! If I get in another attack, I'll receive my first battle stripes. War is half as bad as it sounds and one thing is plain as day: The Russians are fleeing everywhere and we follow them. All of us believe in early victory!*

Dear Mädi, just think of the time when I'll be able to be with you again. Don't worry about me; I will return. Now we must march on. I send my love to you. Kiss my dear son Horsti for me.

Your Papi

*The 7th Panzer Division formed part of the 39th Panzer Corps, an element of Army Group Center's *Panzergruppe 3*. As such it was the left wing of the Army Group's pincers, and saw heavy fighting from the war's first day. Karl was a tank commander and later a platoon leader in the 25th Panzer Regiment, which on 22 June encountered and defeated superior Russian armored forces in what Colonel Rothenburg later called "the hardest fight of his life." On the twenty-fourth, the first elements of the division entered Vilna. (For Operation Barbarossa, see Albert Seaton, *The Russo-German War, 1941–1945* (London, 1971); and his more sharply focused *The Battle for Moscow, 1941–1942* (London, 1971). Bryan Fugate, *Operation Barbarossa: Strategy and Tactics on the Eastern Front, 1941* (Navato, Calif., 1984) is up-to-date and controversial; John Keegan, *Barbarossa: Invasion of Russia, 1941* (New York, 1970) is a useful, popular survey. The best overall treatment is Horst Boog et al., *Der Angriff auf die Sowjetunion*, vol. 4 of *Das Deutsche Reich und der Zweite Weltkrieg* (Stuttgart, 1983). Its 1,100 pages of German academic prose, however, can be expected to daunt all but the hardiest reader.)

*   *   *   *   *

The Eastern Front, Russia

28 June 1941

My dearest wife, my dear little Horsti,

After three days of heavy fighting we were finally granted a well-deserved day of rest. Unfortunately there is some maintenance work that has to be done.

How are you, my two loved ones? Since I received your postcard several days ago, I haven't heard from you. I suppose it's because of the postal delivery which, because of the huge distances now, only comes to us every three or four days. I myself am fine and healthy and today I received my first war decoration from our commander, namely, the tank assault medal.* I wear it proudly and hope you are proud of me.

Up to now, all of the troops have had to accomplish quite a bit. The same goes for our machines and tanks. But, nevertheless, we're going to show those Bolshevik bums who's who around here! They fight like hired hands—not like soldiers, no matter if they are men, women or children on the front lines. They're all no better than a bunch of scoundrels. By now, half of Europe is mobilized. The entry of Spain and Hungary on our side against this Bolshevik archenemy of the world overjoyed us all.** Yes, Europe stands under the leadership of our beloved Führer Adolph Hitler, and he'll reshape it for a better future. The entry of all these volunteer armies into this war will cause the war to be over soon.

The impressions that the battles have left on me will be with me forever. Believe me, dearest, when you see me again, you will face quite a different person, a person who has learned the harsh command: "I will survive!" You can't afford to be soft in war; otherwise you will die. No, you must be tough—indeed, you have to be pitiless and relentless. Don't I sound like a different person to you? Deep down in my heart, I remain a good person and my love for you and our son will never diminish. Never! This love will increase as will my longing for you. I kiss you and remain forever

your Korri

*This decoration was roughly analogous to the U.S. Army's Combat Infantry Badge.

**Spain, in fact, contributed no more than a division of volunteers, never entering the war formally. A significant failure of Nazi diplomacy in 1941 was its inability to mobilize its client states behind a European crusade against Bolshevism. (Cf. Jürgen Förster, "Die Gewinnung von Verbündeten in Südosteuropa," *Angriff auf die Sowjetunion*, 327–64.)

* * * * *

5 July 1941

My darling wife! My dear boy!

We have fought in battle many days now and we have defeated the enemy wherever we have encountered him. Let me tell you that Russia is nothing but misery, poverty and depravity! That is Bolshevism!*

It is late in the evening now and quite dark already. We only wait for our expected orders: Mount your tanks! Start your engines! Move out! Mädi, if you were only here and could see me—tanned by the sun, dusty and dirty, with eyes as clear as a falcon!

Our losses have been minimal and our success is great. This war will be over soon, because already we are fighting against only fragmented opposition.**

How are the two of you? I cannot wait until the moment of my return. It will be wonderful. My return is certain.

Intimate kisses to you, Papi

P.S. Greet your parents and my mother.

*This reaction, common to German soldiers on the Eastern Front in both world wars, contributed not a little to the *Wehrmacht*'s complicity in the

Nazi war of conquest and extermination. Particularly in the summer of 1941, the high-riding *Landser* felt little common humanity toward the peasants whose fields and villages they overran.

**The 7th Panzer Division participated in closing the Minsk pocket, then continued its drive eastward. By 9 July, Army Group Center reported the destruction of twenty-one rifle divisions, fourteen tank brigades, and six motorized brigades, almost two-thirds of the initial opposition. The group tallied over 300,000 prisoners, 2,600 tanks, 1,500 guns—a tremendous victory, yet far from enough to bring the war to an end.

*   *   *   *   *

11 July 1941

Dearest Darling, my dear little Horsti,

Today our united forces captured the Russian city of Vitebsk. It is a large city and has been totally destroyed. Most of the destruction, however, came at the hands of the Russians.* Now we are only several hundred kilometers away from Moscow, and I'm certain that we will soon be in the enemy's capitol. At any rate, these Russian dogs are now on the run. Sometimes I'm tempted to feel sorry for them because many of the soldiers are young boys, hardly sixteen or seventeen years old. But you can't afford to have pity on them.

For the time being I am in a safe spot. If I only had some water to wash myself! The dirt and the dust causes my skin to itch and my beard is growing longer and longer. Wouldn't you like to kiss me now! I'm sure you can see the dirt on the paper on which I write.

While some of us are writing, a couple of other comrades are singing. It's not melodious—I mean they aren't singers—but their song comes from the heart. Here is what they are singing: "Brave little soldier's woman, wait and be patient. Soon I will return to you." I think of you all the time and I kiss and hug you both.

Your Korri

P.S. Please greet your parents and my mother. Are your parents now on vacation in Tyrol or are they still in Nuremberg?

*From the beginning of Operation Barbarossa, the Soviet Union implemented a ruthless scorched-earth policy, destroying what could not be removed.

*   *   *   *   *

15 July 1941

Dearest Darling, my dear little boy,

Finally another day of rest for men and machines! It feels good. You know, on a day like this, you can at least spend some time cleaning everything. For the first time in a long time I have had a chance to take a bath. That was a marvelous, refreshing feeling! My entire body felt like it had been reborn. Before that, however, we had to service our tank, clean it, repair some things, and get it back into tip-top shape. You can't imagine what this dust and dirt does to the machines and to the engines.

We are now positioned outside the city of Smolensk and have penetrated the highly acclaimed Stalin lines. I would imagine that within eight to ten days this campaign will be over. Yes, you can be proud of the German soldiers and the military accomplishments of our men.*

The Russian prisoners all look emaciated. They haven't had anything to eat for days. They, too, are very happy that this war will be over soon. A fellow from the Ukraine was so happy to be taken captive that he almost crushed me while embracing me. I gave him a ride for a couple of miles.

And how are the two of you? I hope you're feeling well. I greet and kiss you.

Your Korri

*Panzergruppe 3, by this time under the command of the 4th Army, continued to drive forward against a virtually new Russian enemy whose divisions, drawn from everywhere in the Soviet Union, gave the Germans an increasingly hard fight all along the high road to Smolensk. Smolensk fell on 15 August, but by then the effect of over-extension on the Wehrmacht was becoming obvious. The armored and motorized spearheads had far outrun the mass of foot-marching infantry and horse-drawn vehicles. Troops had to be diverted to clean up the huge pockets of resistance left behind by the Panzer corps. Tanks and trucks were wearing out and breaking down. The Wehrmacht was beginning to unravel.

*   *   *   *   *

17 July 1941

Sweet Mädi! My dear son!

Yesterday we moved past Smolensk on the city's northern fringe and are now heading toward Moscow. Russian opposition is weak and localized and wherever we meet them, they are forced to flee. Our Air Force, in particular the Stuka attack bombers, actively support our efforts. Our comrades from the Air Force are top-notch guys.*

Yesterday I participated in my twelfth attack. Some of these attacks were more difficult than others. With twelve attacks under my belt, I have now caught up to the boys who had a head start in France! You can imagine that I'm very proud of this achievement. Recent orders have moved us seasoned veterans to the rear so that others have a chance to engage in battle. That makes sense to us, but it wasn't necessarily right because all of us veterans had become accustomed to battle and were at ease on the front line. These newcomers must first earn their seasoned status. . . .**

Mädi, a few words about Russia. All those who today still see any kind of salvation in Bolshevism should be led into this "paradise." To sum it up with one phrase: "It's terrible!" When I get back I will tell you endless horror stories about Russia. Yesterday, for instance, we saw our first women soldiers—Russian women, their hair shorn, in uniform! And these pigs fired on our decent German soldiers from ambush positions.***

. . . In my thoughts I hold you in my arms and kiss your lips and the cheeks of my son.

Your Papi

*At this stage, *Panzergruppe 3* was being supported by arguably the first real tactical air command in history. Wolfram von Richthofen's 7th *Fliegerkorps* was specially organized and trained for direct intervention in the land battle. Time and again its dive bombers and fighters made up for the growing numerical weaknesses of the German ground spearheads.

**The 7th Panzer Division began the campaign with 284 tanks. By 21 July, 166 had been knocked out and one battalion of the 25th Panzer Regiment temporarily broken up to keep the other two approaching effective strength. Most of the crews, however, survived; a shortage of tanks might have accounted for Karl's temporary removal from the front line.

***Every war breeds its tales of Amazons—tales whose psychological implications are more significant than any objective realities behind the accounts themselves. The Red Army did make extensive use of women in frontline units, though usually in support roles, and the 7th Panzer Division captured a number of female auxiliaries in the Smolensk pocket. (For a reproduction of a photograph of one of the prisoners, see von Manteuffel 1965, 171.)

*   *   *   *   *

20 July 1941

My dearest wife, my dear son,

A month ago today we crossed the enemy's border, inspired by our burning desire to beat him wherever we encountered him. With this sacred resolve in mind, we are about to engage in the biggest, most destructive battle ever. What we have accomplished up to now can only be judged by someone who participated in these campaigns. Our division, which reaped so much glory in the West, demonstrated again that it is one of the best. Because of our success, our General received the Knight's Cross from the Führer. We're very proud of our accomplishments.

Today is Sunday and for a change the sun is shining. It had rained heavily in the last couple of days, but now in clear weather our Stuka dive bombers are once again on the prowl. These pilots are really something! Wherever they strike they create havoc and destruction.*

Well, here I sit, lost in thought while I gaze across the wide, monotonous Russian land. My thoughts and wishes travel home to you. I see you, my dearest darling, and I can even see my little boy. As I see you, I feel how much I love you.

Are your parents at home again? Where were you during their vacation? I hope that all of you are in good health. I hug and kiss you.

Love, Korri

*The Stukas' success resulted in large part from the absence of effective fighter or antiaircraft opposition. The vulnerability of the dive bomber, first demonstrated in the Battle of Britain and proved again and again in the Mediterranean, nevertheless did not prevent the *Luftwaffe* from using Stukas effectively against the Russians throughout the war, after 1943 more as a tankbuster than a strike aircraft.

*   *   *   *   *

24 July 1941

Dear Father,

. . . It's been quite a while since you wrote to me and informed me of your transfer. When I received your letter, we were already on the march against the enemy. The weather was incredibly hot, and dust and dirt were our constant companions. From the north of East Prussia we advanced over Kalvarija to Alytus. There I was involved in the biggest tank battle in history! I never believed that I would be able to enter my first battle so calmly. The enemy was thrown back with heavy losses. Immediately we pursued them. On the third day of the campaign we reached Vilnius. The Lithuanian civilians had staged an incredible reception for us. We were literally showered with flowers!*

After a day's rest we continued in the direction of Minsk. I was always up front in my tank, creating gaps in the enemy lines. Special radio announcements reported our accomplishments. When we heard them outside of Minsk, we were overwhelmed. Our company was given special orders and we carried them out to everyone's satisfaction. For a week, during our attack of Lepel and further on in Vitebsk, I was always in the lead with my tank. I will never forget those battle experiences.

Now we are already on the other side of Smolensk. All of my comrades and I who participated in the last twelve attacks have now been taken out of the front lines and given some rest. But I know that I will get my tank back and will get to the front lines again. For me the battle itself is the biggest adventure and experience. During our attack on Minsk I received the Tank Assault Medal and I have been recommended to receive the Iron Cross, Second Class. Yes, we're moving forward towards victory and peace.**

I hope that you are in the best of health. I greet you with our old battle cry: Germany, Sieg Heil!

Your loyal son, Karl

*Lithuania had been under Soviet occupation since the summer of 1940. This brief taste of life dominated by the NKVD (People's Commissariat of Internal Affairs) was more than enough to ensure a warm welcome to the German troops and to inspire a series of vicious pogroms against Vilna's Jews, widely considered Communist sympathizers by their gentile fellow citizens. The *Wehrmacht* saw no reason to intervene.

**The German tanks depended for their early successes on mobility, maneuverability, and accurate shooting far more than on armor or firepower. The 25th Panzer Regiment was at this stage of the war still equipped largely with PzKpfw38(t)'s, a Czech design taken over by the *Wehrmacht*. Weighing only ten tons and armed with a 37-mm gun, it was fast, handy, and mechanically reliable. The regiment also had a few Mark IVs, whose 75-mm gun was a close-support weapon with a barrel so short it was derisively dubbed the "cigar butt." But the German crews were superbly trained—not *all* of the classes about which Karl complained so vociferously had been exercises in paper-pushing. Their commanders were imbued with the spirit of mission tactics and conditioned to taking the initiative instead of waiting for orders. A month of unbroken victory had generated confidence amounting to arrogance at all levels.

*   *   *   *   *

3 August 1941

Dearest Darling, my dear boy,

. . . I've gotten some kind of a rash. I'm continually scratching my entire body. That's how bad it is. I'm blaming the Russian drinking water for it. The water is hardly good enough to wash with, so I guess I really shouldn't drink it.* I can only tell you to be glad that you folks back home don't have to look at this "blessed" Soviet Russia. These scoundrels have been dropping idiotic pamphlets from their airplanes, asking us to surrender our arms and defect to their side. It really is laughable since those bums on the other side surely know that their time is up. All you have to do is look at the Russian prisoners. Hardly ever do you see the face of a person who seems rational and intelligent. They all look emaciated and the wild, half-crazy look in their eyes makes them appear like imbeciles. And these scoundrels, led by Jews and criminals, wanted to imprint their stamp on Europe, indeed on the world. Thank God that our Führer, Adolf Hitler, is preventing this from happening! We're all of the opinion that it is merely a matter of weeks before these Russians will have to give up. Once they do, England will fall as well, and then I will come home to you forever, never to leave again. That's what I long for with all my heart. Hugs and kisses.

Your Korri

*Skin diseases were an increasingly common affliction among tank crews in the summer of 1941—products of water shortages, crowded conditions, dust laden with unfamiliar bacteria and, more obviously, insects. Karl was almost certainly lousy by this time.

* * * * *

3 August 1941

My dear Parents,*

Yesterday I received your second package from Maierhofen.** I really was pleased with the contents. I shared the excellent tobacco and the quality cigarette paper with my comrades since that is the custom. No doubt you, dear Father, remember this custom from the Great War. Cigarettes seem to be soldiers' bread and sometimes they are more important than the food we get. Russian cigarettes are for the birds! Mon Dieu, we would have said in France. But aside from that, we're feeling fine. After six weeks of fighting we've become accustomed to combat and so it doesn't bother us anymore. Artillery fire or even an occasional inaccurately thrown bomb from the enemy doesn't disturb us. We've become stoic and I guess you could say that we are simply "old" soldiers. This war against these sub-human beings is about over. It's almost insulting when you consider that drunken Russian criminals have been let loose against us. We really let them have it! They are scoundrels, the mere scum of the earth! Naturally they are not a match for us German soldiers. Not even their biggest tanks can protect them.

A few simple birch crosses speak of the heroism of our comrades. We have decorated these graves with the soldiers' steel helmets or with the black cap of the tank troops. They gave their lives for Germany and for those of us who are alive, there is only one motto: Fight on to the final victory!

My hearty greetings and Sieg Heil.

Your Karl

*Letter to his in-laws.

**Vacation village in Tyrol.

* * * * *

4 August 1941

Dear Father,

From your letter of June 20th I can see that you are busy with important assignments. Perhaps you've been reassigned and are now close to me in Russia. Yes, your prediction of my "baptism of fire" has come true.

The change in me from a "home" soldier to a frontline soldier was so sudden that I hardly noticed the transition. From the very first shot on, the choice was a simple one: It's either the enemy or me! That's been my motto from the start; you simply can't afford to think in war. Contemplation could cause your death. On the contrary, you must take aim at the enemy, keep your finger on the trigger and come hell or high water, you must keep self-preservation uppermost in your mind. You can imagine that we have pulled off a couple of nifty stunts, especially with the help of you guys in the Air Force. We've really gotten to know the flyboys in this war. Without exception they are top-notch guys and bring death and destruction to the enemy.

The pitiful hordes on the other side are nothing but felons who are driven by alcohol and the threat of pistols pointed at their heads. There is no troop morale and they are at best cannon fodder.* You should read the pamphlets that they drop from the sky with better accuracy than their bombs. "Desert! Join the Bolsheviks! You'll be safe with us!" They are nothing but a bunch of assholes! Excuse the expression, but there simply is no other term for them. Having encountered these Bolshevik hordes and having seen how they live has made a lasting impression on me. Everyone, even the last doubter, knows today that the battle against these subhumans, who've been whipped into a frenzy by the Jews, was not only necessary but came in the nick of time. Our Führer has saved Europe from certain chaos.

And so we move on to the final battle and victory. I shake your hand and greet you. Germany, Sieg Heil!

Your loyal son, Karl

*Prisoners of war seldom look as though they are ready for a formal inspection, particularly in the eyes of their captors. Karl's comments, however, indicate the *Wehrmacht*'s ready acceptance of Hitler's racially based ideologies. The mishandling of Russian prisoners by the *Wehrmacht*, as well as by the SS, is established in Christian Streit, *Keine Kameraden* (Wiesbaden, 1978).

German accounts from this period are rife with descriptions of Russian counterattacks fueled by alcohol and sustained by threats of being shot from behind. Russian narratives describe "a necessary strengthening of discipline" and purging of "defeatist elements." Although by this time the Russian army's supply of trained manpower has been sorely depleted, the history of the 7th Panzer Division belies Karl's contempt for his enemy. From 27 July to 6 August, Karl's unit was under constant Russian counterattacks. The situation frequently became "extremely critical"—critical enough that the artillery men had to defend their battery position with rifles and hand grenades (von Manteuffel, 171–172).

*　*　*　*　*

15 August 1941

My dearest Mädi, my little Horsti,

Last night we had a little party for a number of comrades who've been reassigned back to the Fatherland. In the midst of the celebration we sang some German folk songs under the Russian sky. Our songs sounded almost like prayers in this wretched Russian land. While we sang, our native Germany materialized in front of us. Our homeland seemed more magnificent and beautiful than ever before. Our thoughts traveled west towards home, to wife and child, to parents and sisters, to all of those for whom we fight out here. What great strength can be found in German song! Even if we have to do without a lot of things out here, no one can take those magnificent songs away from us.

My darling, we've been camping out under the open sky for weeks now. We have slept in our tanks, we have bedded down at night without a roof over us, and for the time being we are holed up in tents. We have forgotten what a house and a nicely furnished room looks like. We no longer have an inkling what comfort is, because since the beginning of this campaign we haven't seen any comfortable rooms or houses. No matter where you look, there is nothing but dirty, filthy block houses. You can't find a trace of culture anywhere. We now realize what our great

German Fatherland has given its children. There exists only one Germany in the entire world. . . .

In love and loyalty,

Your Korri

Attitudes like Karl's contributed as much as soldiers' comradeship or party slogans to the extraordinary endurance demonstrated by the Germans on the Russian front. Contempt for alien ways seems virtually a universal characteristic of armies—particularly in the combat units, which are not usually manned by cosmopolitan intellectuals. For the *Wehrmacht*'s rank and file, a vague, centuries-old, sense of defending the West from Slavic barbarism was reinforced by direct experience of a culture that seemed at once incomprehensibly alien and overwhelmingly threatening to Germans whose provincialism had been fostered and reinforced by National Socialism. Karl Fuchs's Russian counterparts had been exposed to an ideology and political system that encouraged them to think of themselves, however vaguely, as part of the vanguard of an international movement. National Socialism correspondingly fostered a sense of cultural isolation. For many of its adherents its Utopian visions were of an endlessly extended Rosstal. (For an alternate interpretation, stressing the direct influence of Nazi ideology and propaganda, see Omer Bartov, *The Eastern Front, 1941–45: German Troops and the Barbarisation of Warfare* (New York, 1986).)

*   *   *   *   *

16 August 1941

Dear Father,

I was extremely pleased to finally receive a letter from you. At least I now know that you are alive and well and stationed in a new place. Your letter was underway from the 27th of June until the 15th of July. That in itself, I guess, is an indication of how great the distance is between us now. For a while I thought you were still in the West.* I asked every air defense soldier I ran into about you, but no one could tell me anything about your whereabouts.

A few days ago I was up front again because the front unit was a tank short. So once again I was engaged in a spearhead attack. At the conclusion of this skirmish, my boss decorated me with the Iron Cross, Second Class. Naturally, I'm very proud of this decoration and I now wear the black, white and red ribbon next to my Tank Assault Medal.

No matter where the enemy is, it is certain that we will beat him. Dear Father, we have fought against Russian tanks which seemed invincible because of their armor plating; however, our enthusiasm and spirited attack beat them every time.** You know what bad shape the Russian tank units are in today and much of that is due to our aggressive attacks. Come what may, we have only one thing in mind and that is to fight and to win.

Remain healthy and Sieg Heil.

Your loyal son, Karl

*Hans Fuchs was transferred from France to Russia in June 1941. On his way to his new assignment he was able to visit Mädi and his new grandson in Rosstal.

**Karl is referring here to the KV heavy tank. It existed in two versions. The KV I weighed 46 or 47 tons and mounted a 76-mm gun. The 53-ton KV II mounted a 152-mm howitzer in a bulky, slab-sided turret. Clumsily handled by inexperienced crews, they nevertheless shocked the Germans by their virtual invulnerability to existing tank and antitank guns at ranges as short as fifty to a hundred yards. To knock them out it was necessary to maneuver to their flank or rear, taking advantage of the thin armor there.

* * * * *

22 August 1941

My dearest Darling, my little boy,

The triumphant sounds of marches resonate throughout the forest in which we are presently camped. These are mighty and glorious sounds with the fanfares of the trumpet seeming to announce imminent victory. No, this is no dream, but our regimental band is playing today. The heavy, solid harmony of this music gives you the necessary strength to carry on. When I hear and feel this music, I'm always jubilant.*

What an immense contrast this Russian land is to our homeland! The people here can't give you anything because they have nothing—they possess nothing. Sometimes we feel lonely in this vast land. You should hear how fervently we sing our simple folk songs, hoping that you at home can hear them.

I have been reading some books lately. Yesterday, for instance, I finished a beautiful novel entitled *Heather Schoolmaster*

Uwe Karsten. Do you know this novel? Are you familiar with the great figure of this teacher and his ceaseless love and longing for his home? The language is wonderful and I spent some happy hours reading the book.** I must read in order to have any intellectual stimulus in this desolate land.

I think of you every day and I never go to sleep without looking at your picture. Then I can fall asleep peacefully and serenely because I know that you, with your loving heart, with your prayers and your belief in me, protect me. I believe more than ever before that one day soon the world will be a better, more beautiful place than ever before. Please rock our boy in your arms and tell him of his father who loves him so much.

Love and kisses, Korri

*Even under the increasingly desperate manpower shortages, German regiment and divisional commanders tried to maintain bands, whose positive effects on morale is frequently affirmed by *Wehrmacht* veterans. Singing has been of enduring importance in the German army, owing to a longstanding institutional conviction that singing made long marches easier and fostered group identity.

**Rose Moersberger's novel, published in 1920, belonged to that genre of *Heimatromane,* sentimental works glorifying the simple life of Germany's traditional countryside, that flourished from the 1890s into the 1930s. Most of the works were innocuous in themselves, but provided fertile soil for *völkische* and Nazi ideas. (Cf. the detailed treatment in Karlheinz Rossbacher, *Heimatkunstbewegung und Heimatroman* (Stuttgart, 1975).)

*   *   *   *   *

24 August 1941

My dear Mother,

I want to thank you very much for your letter of August 9th. You, Mädi, and others at home write to me so nicely about my little boy that everytime I hear about him, I become very happy and proud. These dear words mean so much to me out here at the front, so far away from home. I'm very pleased to hear that our child has created some harmony and love at home.

Today is Sunday. It's really a day like any other day, but nevertheless it seems to be a holiday for me because not only did I get your letter, but also one from my wife that included three pictures of Horsti. I guess tomorrow Mädi will start teaching again in Rosstal. Do you know, Mother, how much I long to be back teaching my elementary school students? Just thinking about it makes me happy.

Soon this war out here will be over and then we will all live in peace and happiness. We'll be able to devote our time to the future of our children, and that's why I gladly sacrifice my time and energy during this war. In spite of the battles, however, my thoughts often travel homeward and then I'm able to picture my homeland, my Franconia, with all the things that I love about it.

Please greet everyone at home! For you I will always be

your loyal son, Karl

* * * * *

27 August 1941

My dear Father,

A few days ago the tanks were started up again and they rumbled towards the front. We shook hands with our comrades and off they went. Some of us, me included, are recuperating several kilometers behind the front line and are staying in one of these endless, monotonous Russian forests. It certainly is a strange feeling for me to be here and not in the midst of the fighting. But our company commander is of the opinion that, if possible, all members of the company should have the opportunity to fight at the front.

Our losses so far have been minimal. This is due to excellent leadership and magnificent soldiering spirit. The Bolsheviks, however, who are under tremendous political pressure to win, are defending themselves desperately and their morale is low. Their losses are heavy. We're of the opinion that it's only a matter of weeks now until the final battles around St. Petersburg and in the Ukraine will be fought. We have news from the Ukraine that Gomel has fallen and we are overjoyed.* What will the world say when England, in spite of this immense Russian battlefront, receives its knockout blow? All I can say here is poor Churchill and Roosevelt! I'm convinced that the Russian army, decimated and beaten, will be destroyed by the end of this year.

I'm very glad that my biggest worry, namely, troubles at

home, has finally been solved. Mädi started teaching school again on the 25th of August and apparently she and Mother are now getting along well. They are quite concerned about our little boy. I'm mighty proud of him and can't wait to see him! I'm looking forward to the day when you, Uncle Willi and I can drink to him while playing cards back home at the Eckert Inn. In the meantime, however, duty calls and our motto is: For Führer and Germany! I shake your hand and know that I'm looking into proud eyes.

Your loyal son, Karl

*On 16 August, the 7th Panzer Division, with the rest of the 39th Panzer Corps, was transferred to Army Group North to support its attack on Leningrad. The drive on Moscow now became proportionally contingent on Army Group North's success. Army Group Center was to shift to the defensive, with most of its remaining armored forces assigned to Army Group South to expedite capture of the Donets Basin and the Crimea. This decision, made by Hitler over the strenuous objection of the army high command, reflected the dictator's growing conviction that a decisive victory in 1941 was no longer possible. The generals' insistence that it represented amateurish dispersion of forces in part reflected their own wishful thinking; the *Wehrmacht*'s heavy losses in men and equipment were making the possibility of a successful drive on Moscow increasingly unlikely. From a frontline perspective, however, Army Group South's triumphs in the Ukraine in the aftermath of Hitler's order seemed one long step closer to home.

*   *   *   *   *

28 August 1941

My dearest Mädi,

Today I have to send all your correspondence back to you because it is now forbidden to take letters to the front. I'm going to send them in four envelopes.* I'll send two envelopes to you, one to your mother in Nuremberg, and the fourth I will address to my mother. Please take good care of these letters because they were, especially after the difficult hours in battle, a source of much joy and pleasure to me. Of course, you know what I intend to do with them once I return; I want to use them as a resource for my literary project.

Oh, Mädi, once I'm back with you, I will get straight to

work. All my work will be for you and for little Horsti. The letter that I received from you yesterday included two enlarged photographs of our little son. I can't believe how sweet he is! I love you very much.

Your Korri

*These letters have been lost.

*   *   *   *   *

2 September 1941

My dearest Darling, my dear little Horsti,

It is already September and fall has come. The arrival of fall wasn't exactly pleasant because it's been raining cats and dogs since yesterday. The raindrops are drumming on our tent and we're very happy that the tent is located on a high, dry spot. We built up the ground beneath it so that the water runs off well. At the same time, this protects us from the cold which at night now is quite noticeable.*

When night falls the three of us, all noncoms, huddle close together and speak about our loved ones at home and about our Fatherland. Our language is simple—it's the language of comrades. Our words come from the heart and carry a lot of emotion. Sometimes we even sing one of our beautiful old folk songs and these sometimes sound like prayers. After that we're happy and serene. I ask myself when I will be able to go home. But I must not give this thought much priority even though it is my deepest wish.

On Sunday, the day before yesterday, I read another Schroer book entitled *The Avalanche of St. Thomas*. I haven't told you, but I'm in charge of our small library here and I find great pleasure in this job. Nothing is more stimulating in this monotonous Russia than a good book. Sometimes on weekend mornings I even instruct my comrades in history and geography. Every now and then I have enthusiastic listeners. Well, you have to do what you can to keep your mind active out here.

Yesterday I sent off the promised money for Horsti. I hope that you have received the other 200 RM by now. I, in turn, have received your little care package and want to thank you very much for it.

It's raining harder now and darkness has fallen. I greet you and kiss you.

Your Korri

*The role of "General Winter" in Operation Barbarossa has been frequently exaggerated by *Wehrmacht* apologists. Nevertheless, RHS Stolfi has recently demonstrated that the winter of 1941, earlier than usual and much more severe than could have been anticipated, did significantly influence the course of operations. (See "Chance in History: The Russian Winter of 1941–1942, *History 65* (1980), 219–28.)

* * * * *

2 September 1941

My dear Mother,

September has brought us bad weather. Mädi has probably told you all about the rain since I wrote to her about it. All I can say is that Russia is like a big pigsty! It's an incredible country! When you take into consideration our recent achievements and successes in battle, you can't help but believe that this war will be over at the end of this year.* Rewal has fallen! Leningrad is encircled! We have had tremendous successes in the South! The achievements of the army have been so magnificent that one can certainly look with great pride upon them. No matter how the Russian soldiers defend themselves, they have had it! They're desperate and right now are driven towards the front with threats from their political commissars. Their last hour has come!

I often look at the pictures of my little boy and become incredibly happy. Horsti is already three months old and I, his father, haven't even seen him. You must understand that I'm yearning to see my little boy and to get back to my family. Nevertheless, the duty towards our Fatherland is more important at the moment. It is also a sacred duty and we all know that we're fighting for the existence and survival of our people.

Stay healthy and greet everyone in Rosstal.

Your son, Karl

*Now Tallin, Estonia. A Russian "Dunkirk" took place there.

* * * * *

3 September 1941

My dear Father,

In these last three weeks, a lot of things have happened and our comrades in the South, especially in the Ukraine, have experienced successes and have caught up with our push to the East. I wish you could have been here when we heard that Rewal had fallen.* God, were we overjoyed! I guess the strength of the German soldier is unique and it seems that he is invincible. You and I wouldn't be two of a kind if we didn't have the exact same feelings about these victories. I can imagine that you would be a great leader of our outfit! I will never forget how the eyes of all my comrades lit up when, for the first time, orders for battle were given: Start the engines of your tanks! That's all we had been waiting for and once we started, we pursued and defeated the enemy wherever we met him. Not one of us thought of death in battle. Unfortunately, some of my best friends have been killed. Nevertheless, all of us have only one thought in mind—to defeat the enemy. I saw men weep who had lost their tanks in battle and I'll never forget how they attacked Russian tanks with weapons in their hands. A country such as ours that has men like these must live forever.

Mother wrote to me today and congratulated me on my achievements. Here's what she said: "My dear boy! I, as your mother, want to congratulate you for the decoration which you, as an honorable and brave soldier, received." When Mother writes like that we know that our loved ones at home believe in what we are doing and support us completely. That means a lot for us men out here. They shouldn't complain at home but should be proud of us. The life of the individual is insignificant compared to the history that is being made today.

I want to greet you with "Germany, Sieg Heil."

Your loyal son, Korri

*This major naval base and Baltic port fell to the German 42d Corps on

28 August. To the men in the ranks it seemed the last barrier before Leningrad.

*   *   *   *   *

7 September 1941

My dearest wife! Little Horsti!

Another Sunday—a quiet, lonely day like so many others. Time marches on and you don't even realize that with each passing day you get older. So here I sit, rather contemplative, in my neat, clean tent. The sun is out (probably because it's Sunday) and its rays warm the tent roof.

We've been camping out in this country now for eleven weeks and every day has brought something different: sometimes there are shouts of joy because of our mighty victories; at other times there is mourning because of our dead and wounded comrades—but always honest pride. All of us are guided by a beacon, and this guiding light is a belief in victory. Everything is possible with this belief in our hearts.* The actual experience of war is an overpowering one and your feelings during the battle are many-sided and unfathomable. I've tried to keep a diary and want to elaborate on them at a later date. . . . I know your love will protect me.

Love, Korri

*This attitude so often repeated in Karl's letters is more than abstract rhetoric or youthful enthusiasm. The *Wehrmacht* was permeated from top to bottom by a kind of military vitalism, stressing morale factors, as opposed to physical and material considerations. It antedated the Nazi era, being in large part a product of World War I and its aftermath—a period in which German military doctrine stressed the importance of intangibles. It has been contrasted sharply with the U.S. army's managerial approach by such scholars as Martin van Creveld and Russell Weigley. But, while morale factors may considerably enhance fighting power, they will not make their possessors bulletproof and cannot compensate entirely for numerical or technical inferiority. Far too often, even in the early stages of Barbarossa, Germany's commanders put an almost mystical faith in the ability of the man on the front line to surmount any difficulty by ingenuity and force of will.

*   *   *   *   *

10 September 1941

Dearest Darling, dear little Horsti,

Although it's only 6:00 p.m., dusk has already settled over our campsite. An hour from now it will be quite dark. We will then gather again around the campfire and sing a few of our beautiful German folk songs.

Yesterday I had the opportunity to visit the city of Smolensk.* Although I gathered many impressions there, let me just tell you of one. I was able to visit a former orthodox cathedral. The interior of this cathedral was richly decorated with gold and other artifacts and I doubt that you could find such a magnificent church anywhere else in the world. The Bolsheviks, however, have altered this cathedral considerably and have turned it into an anti-God museum. It is really disgusting how these Communist scoundrels treat everything that is great and holy. If you had a chance to observe these Russians with their distorted, grimacing faces, driven by a political insanity, then you would feel the same kind of rage which I felt after I had walked into that church. In my opinion, these Bolsheviks are murderers of all culture!

I have just finished two more books. One was called *Walter von Plettenberg* and is about the struggles and battles of the German knights against the frightful destruction of Russia under Ivan the Terrible, the bloody Czar. It is indeed a powerful novel. The other book was *Hermann Göring, the Man and his Work*. It wasn't really a biography, but more of a novel that depicted this man and fighter as he was—the story of a real national socialist.**

I'm including two letters that you ought to keep in your file. When you read them, you will be able to form your own opinion about things out here.***

Darkness is slowly settling over our forest. I'd like to sing quietly for you—for you alone—and Richard Strauss's eternal melody comes to mind: "Silently we will gaze in each others' eyes and happiness will come over us."****

In true love, Your Korri

*Smolensk was captured by the Germans before it could be destroyed.

**Karl's second reference is to Erich Gritzbach's official biography, *Hermann Göring: Werk und Mensch* (Munich, 1938). His one-sentence evaluation of the work was more perceptive than those of several subsequent historians who took Gritzbach literally. (See Richard P. Hamilton, "Hermann Göring's First Public Address: A Note on 'Popular' History," *Canadian Journal of History/Annales Canadiennes d'Histoire 19* (1984), 201–16.)

***These letters have been lost. Frau Fuchs affirms that nothing in her husband's correspondence was anomalous; there is no reason to assume that these items contained any unexpected revelations about Karl's war.

****"Morgen" (Opus 27, Song 4) by Richard Strauss.

* * * * *

13 September 1941

My dearest wife, my little Horsti,

Rain is again falling on our tent. Because of the constant rain the pathways of this country, which they call streets, are becoming impassable. You can't imagine what terrible shape they're in.* I don't know what's going to happen when, in a few weeks, the bad weather period is supposed to start! Since we're no longer directly engaged in battle, we have much time to think of our comrades up front who, in their foxholes filled with water and dirt, are lying there with their guns aimed at the enemy. Their tenacity speaks of the courage and readiness of the German soldier!

Starting last night, I began to have some cramps in my stomach. It must be some kind of intestinal flu, but I feel better now.

For the time being there's nothing I'd rather do out here than read. I suddenly have an incredible urge to read and to become more educated. I've almost completed a long novel and am sure that it will have a lasting effect on me. This book is called *The Lion* by Mirco Jalusich and is about the history, unity, and greatness of Germany during the time of Heinrich, the Lion. He is a magnificent and noble figure.

Yes, once the fighting is over and we are together again, we must study German history and literature together. I'm looking forward to those evenings where we will find each other in art and history during hours of intellectual activity. I know that we will stimulate and encourage each other in this pastime. Yes, my dearest, our married life will never be monotonous. I have learned out here what monotony is and I've had enough of it. That's why I am longing to teach again. I miss my elementary school students very much and would like to be able to enthuse and enlighten them about many things. It seems to me that I can do this best in those subjects which I have chosen as my major. The battle out here, which I have fought for us, has matured me considerably. I kiss you on your white forehead.

Your loyal Korri

*The 7th Panzer Division by this time was operating well away from any of the few paved roads in north Russia and used its tracked vehicles, including tanks, to sustain logistic mobility.

* * * * *

17 September 1941

My dearest Mädi,

My hands are so cold that I can hardly write to you. Thank God we're on the move again and about to camp at another location.* I can tell you that the roads are in terrible condition. There's mud everywhere and the rain doesn't seem to want to stop. Horses would probably be of more use to us now than vehicles.** Sometimes we have to make new roads by simply driving across the countryside. But everywhere you go you slip and slide and get stuck.

If you happen to have some woolen gloves and a woolen scarf, please send these items to me. I don't even know if I still have gloves and a scarf at home.*** In a few weeks we expect it to get very cold here.

Dear Mädi, yesterday I had such a longing for you. I had to literally suppress my tears. Please kiss my boy and I remain,

Your Korri

Greetings to my mother.

*Since 17 August, the 7th Panzer Division had been out of the line for rest and reinforcement. On 17 September, it began moving forward to a deployment area around Sloboda, thirty-five kilometers northeast of Demidov (von Manteuffel, 185).

**Even motorized formations were beginning to acquire horses locally to supplement the trucks that so quickly became hopelessly bogged down in the mud, and to spare their overworked tracked vehicles.

***The well-documented failure to equip the *Wehrmacht* for a Russian winter resulted from the generals' overconfidence, as well as Hitler's. As late as November, the men of 7th Panzer were ordered to make white camouflage clothing from local resources. Since sheets and pillowcases were not common items in Stalin's Russia, most of the riflemen donned what remained of their underwear over their field-gray uniforms (von Manteuffel, 214).

* * * * *

22 September 1941

My dearest Mädi,

Our German proverb, "different people have different customs," does not apply to this endless, monotonous country of Russia. I suppose this proverb may be applicable to many countries on earth, but not here. This country, like its people, seems eternally gray and monotonous. Everywhere you look there is nothing but poverty and wretched misfortune. Poverty looks at you from every corner, and certainly the men, women and children are terribly poor. Can you imagine that human beings grow up to live like animals? That seems to be the case here. Just the other day I mentioned to one of my comrades that even a little flower in God's wonderful nature grows up with more sunshine during its lifetime and enjoys more care and happiness than these people here. It would be inconceivable for me to have our child live in such an environment! I suppose it's just as impossible to ask a Russian to think of something beautiful and noble.*

If you only knew under what arduous conditions our victories were fought and won. Sometimes it was incredible, fighting on muddy Russian roads or in rainy weather that seemed to have no end. Time and space are suspended. Once this last battle is over, peace will return to Germany and Europe. We out here on the front carry this belief in our hearts. You back home should have the same belief and hope as we do. Due to this common belief and hope, the front and the homeland are united in the real sense of the word. This point of view should play an important part in the schools today. You as teachers who are able to mold and educate the youth of our great country should, in this difficult and proud time, let our children participate in the heroism of their brothers and fathers. I would give anything if I were able to stand in front of my elementary school students for just one day.** A teacher must be enthusiastic and must have a burning desire to teach. If he can do this, he has the undivided attention of his pupils and doesn't have to worry about discipline. Believe me, all the things that I have learned out here in this monumental struggle will help me become a better teacher.

You probably are spending much time with our son. Your entire love must belong to this child since it is our child. But when you are teaching school, you must also share this love and enthusiasm with your pupils. Otherwise you should quit your job. I've become very conscious of the fact that our teaching profession, especially today and after the war, will demand real idealists. You can't do this job well if you do it half-heartedly.

I hope everything is in order at home and no one is quarreling. Always think of us out here on the front who are protecting you, if need be with our lives. When you think of this, then you must agree that the little quarrels that occur at home once in a while between family members are only secondary. Hug my child and kiss him for me.

With all my love, Your Korri

*Though Karl's regiment was fighting its way through some of European Russia's most backward regions, his observations are shared almost universally among Barbarossa's veterans. Their opinion was most harsh during the first summer, before the Germans learned that many features of Russian peasant life resulted from environmental conditions different even from those in eastern Germany. Nevertheless, the militant anti-Communist attitude of so many survivors of the Russian front was a product of direct experience as well as indoctrination. To a significant extent, the war in the east was a war of toothbrushes and plumbing fixtures.

**For a description of frontline soldiers visiting schools at the home front, see chapters 5 and 7 of Günter Grass's prose work *Cat and Mouse*. Grass's perspective of the educational value of such visits is sufficiently different from Karl's to warrant mentioning here.

*　*　*　*　*

26 September 1941

My dear Father,

It seems that you are now stationed much farther away from me than I had initially assumed. I haven't heard a word from you in weeks. Perhaps you were participating in the monumental battle of encirclement around Kiev and thus were unable to write.* If you were there, I assure you that our tank battalion will vie with you for this glory. Yes, thank God, I have a new tank and am waiting for my orders. My tank crew and I are eager to move out and we're itching to prove ourselves once more in battle. Once the last battle is fought and won out here on the Russian front, those fellows on the other side of the English Channel will really get worried. We can hear them already, lying, foaming at the mouth, and inciting others against us. None of that will help those British scoundrels. Once the German sword strikes, they will be hurting for sure.

My God, you can't believe how proud we are of our Fatherland and how often we long to be back in our homeland, to see its forests and meadows, its lakes and mountains. Let me greet you with Germany, Sieg Heil!

Your loyal son, Karl

*The Panzer divisions diverted to Army Group South from Army Group Center formed the northern arm of a pincer that enclosed the city of Kiev and almost three-quarters of a million Russian troops. The encirclement was completed on 15 September. Kiev fell four days later. By 25 September the battle was over. The Germans took 650,000 prisoners. Their hopes of a successful attack on Moscow were renewed.

* * * * *

9 October 1941

My dearest Mädi, my dear little boy,

I'm sure that you must have heard the special radio announcements about our battle achievements.* Yes, you can find me somewhere on this front near Moscow! The Russians didn't believe that we would attack at this time of the year when the cold weather is setting in. They probably thought that we would give them a recuperative period until next year. The last hour of Bolshevism is near and that means that Old England's destruction is imminent. You can hear on that island now the same desperate cries which once were uttered in ancient Rome: "Germani ante portas," and this time it's Adolf Hitler who is standing before the gates. These are my comments about the present political situation.

For the time being, we are resting in a Russian blockhouse. Since it is terribly cold and unfriendly outside, we have no choice but to move inside and fight it out with the lice. Don't be afraid when I come home in a few weeks, my darling, I won't bring any of these bugs along. The only thing that I'll bring is myself. Is that enough for you? Can you sense how much I need you from the letters that I've been writing or has my language become too difficult and somber? I'm still thinking about the rather incomprehensible sentences that you wrote in your letter of the 13th of last month. It sounded like you are starting to distrust me! I didn't know what you meant. I certainly keep no secrets from you. Are you perhaps somewhat jealous of me? I assure you, I belong to you alone. I'm not going to become upset about those few comments because I know that you will write me soon and tell me what you meant.

In two days our child will be four months old. In these four months I have been separated from you and have been with you only in my thoughts. All of us believe and trust the words of the Führer in his great speech. Indeed, the last decisive battle stands before us. Soon I will be home to hug and kiss you and then I will finally hold my baby boy in my arms.

Your Korri

Please greet Mother, your parents and all our other friends for me.

---

*The 7th Panzer Division, now part of *Panzergruppe 3*'s 61st Panzerkorps, spearheaded Operation Typhoon, the German offensive against Moscow. The division attacked on 2 October. Closely supported by the Stukas of the 8th *Fliegerkorps,* its 25th Panzer Regiment reached and crossed the Dnieper the next day and cut the high road to Moscow on 6 October. As part of a pincers formed with *Panzergruppe 4,* transferred from the Leningrad front, Karl's division helped encircle large Russian forces around Vyazma. Further south, Heinz Guderian's *Panzergruppe 2* took Orel on 2 October and Bryansk on 7 October. Six-hundred-fifty-thousand Russians were trapped in the resulting pockets. On 8 October, Chief of Staff Franz Halder confidently predicted that reasonably good weather and reasonably good leadership would win the Germans Moscow in the near future.

*   *   *   *   *

12 October 1941

Dear Father,

Didn't I predict this news? You must have heard the special announcements about Vyazma. Yes, you can find me here. I almost think that this battle is the last flickering moment of a once powerful Russia. For days now the enemy has tried to break out of our iron encirclement, but their efforts have been in vain. Wherever there is a hot spot, we appear like ghosts and engage the enemy in battle. Yesterday must have been our company's proudest day in this campaign. The alarm sounded and our tanks moved out! Russian tanks reinforced with support troops wanted to break out of our ring. My unit (and I'm its temporary commander) was assigned the task of scouting the opposition. Visibility was low because of ground fog. We moved four tanks into an advantageous position. Suddenly three heavy Russian tanks, big as battleships, appeared out of the fog to the right of us. We opened fire immediately, but these tanks had enormous armor plating. If they had known that only four tiny scout tanks were opposing them! But here as well, courage and audacity brought us victory. Two of their tanks were burning and the third pulled away. Once the fog lifted from the valley, we really let them have it with every barrel. Tanks, antiaircraft guns, trucks and the infantry fired on everything in sight. Once the main body of our company arrived, our comrades destroyed their remaining forces. Proud and satisfied, our company commander smiled at us while our eyes were still flashing. We had no losses at all. My cap, though, had a five centimeter tear in it, due to a splinter.*

In the evening, civilians helped us reload our machine guns. You cannot imagine how glad they were to have been freed of

Bolshevism.** You can see that we are prepared at all times to beat the enemy wherever he may appear!

Germany Sieg Heil!

Your loyal son, Karl

I haven't received any mail from you in six weeks.

*From platoon to army group, the Germans' superiority on the eastern front depended heavily on the flexibility of their command structure and the initiative of their frontline leaders. The 7th Panzer Division's history describes these characteristics during the Vyazma *Kesselschlacht* without specifically mentioning Karl's little skirmish and its improbable results. Karl's adversaries were the KV I tanks described earlier.

**This incident is still another indication of the goodwill the Nazi occupiers destroyed through their ideologically based, racist policies.

* * * * *

15 October 1941

My dearest Darling! My boy!

It is snowing and a carpet of pure white covers the earth, the earth which has drunk so much red blood.* My brave, young friend Roland just died of severe wounds. Why did he have to give his life now, with the end practically in sight? We hard-hearted soldiers have no time to bemoan his fate. We tie down our helmets and think of revenge, revenge for our dead comrades. The battle of Vyazma is over and the last elite troops of the Bolsheviks have been destroyed.** I will never forget my impressions of this destruction. From now on, their opposition will not be comparable to previous encounters. All we have to do now is roll on, for the opposition will be minor.

But that's enough talk about war. Let's talk about tomorrow, about the future which hopefully will bring an early peace.

The last letter from you, as a matter of fact the last news from home, is over a month old. I guess the mail can't catch up with us any more. No doubt it takes a while for letters to reach home as well. But I beg you, don't fear for me because I will return home. What all of us fear most now is the snow and the accompanying cold temperatures, but we'll get used to it. It won't last much longer. Right now our activities are about as dangerous as if we were on a mere expedition.

It's continuing to snow outside. The covering of snow across this immense land brings with it a certain pre-Christmas spirit. Last night in my dreams I was at home with you, preparing for Christmas, the feast of love and peace. I was so close to you and then I awakened. One day my dream will come true. You must feel how much I love you.

Korri

*The first snowfall in the Vyazma-Bryansk area occurred on 6 and 7 October. The cold and frost were frequently accepted in the combat units as a welcome alternative to the mud that had so handicapped the German mobile forces in the preceding month.

**The Russian 3d Army surrendered at Vyazma on 14 October. The 32d Army held out around Bryansk six days longer.

*   *   *   *   *

15 October 1941

My dear Mother,

While a terrible snowstorm is howling outside, my comrades and I are camping in one of these terrible peasant houses. Although it's not much of a home, we managed to clean it up yesterday. Up until now we've always preferred to dig a hole in the ground and maybe pitch a tent. Now, however, it's simply too cold outside. If you could see how these people live here, you would be horrified!

This present abode is in better shape than most. In one corner there is even a structure that looks like a bed. Most Russians don't sleep in beds, but either behind or on top of their stove. I won't describe the other facilities, such as water and sanitation. Suffice it to say that they hardly exist.

Our duty has been to fight and to free the world from this Communist disease. One day, many years hence, the world will thank the Germans and our beloved Führer for our victories here in Russia. Those of us who took part in this liberation battle can look back on those days with pride and infinite joy. That's all for today. I send you my greetings.

Your son, Karl

* * * * *

20 October 1941

My dearest Darling, my little happy boy,

Looking outside you'd think that I was writing this letter in the middle of the night, but when I look at the clock I see that it is only 8:30 p.m. It's been dark for hours because in the winter months darkness comes early to these regions. Furthermore, it has been raining again and an unexpected thaw has set in. The formerly white cover of snow has turned dirty brown and mud and slush are everywhere. We drive our vehicles across the fields and leave deep furrows behind. Frequently the vehicles slip and slide and even get stuck. We have lost all sense of time and don't know what day it is or what time it is. The early gray of the morning, which penetrates through the small windows of our bunker, indicates the coming of a new day, and the dusk that seems to settle in soon thereafter heralds the coming night. This cycle seems to be an endless one. In between the changes is an endless monotony. The landscape here is bleak and desolate. If we weren't here to fight and were only here to live—I mean to exist here—we would become imbeciles. Now that we have been here for some time and have had a chance to become acquainted with this land, we all of a sudden understand why it was an easy thing for the Communist agitators to systematically poison these people.

We've been hanging around here for days.* If we only had something to read. We've gone through all the magazines a dozen times. We've solved all the crossword puzzles and we've done it over and over again only to be entertained a little bit.

Please save my letters because I want to read them again when I return. These letters are but sketches, but I will remember from them the true character of this country and its people who have been so depraved by these idiotic Communist ideas. Experiencing the conditions in which they're forced to live will remain with me forever. We Germans can hardly breathe in this atmosphere. Their houses are oppressive. Certainly we couldn't live here. And the lice are terrible.**

It has gotten late and I still want to write a little note to Mother. You perhaps are sleeping right now with our child. Sleep deeply and peacefully. Your Korri is guarding you out here on the eastern front.

Love and kisses, Korri

*The German offensive was by this time stalled by a combination of the bad weather Karl describes and an increasing crisis in supply and reinforcements. By 16 October, Army Group Center had suffered 277,000 casualties and received only 151,000 replacements. Companies and battalions were at less than half, sometimes less than a third, of their authorized strength. The 7th Panzer Division was withdrawn for reorganization on 13 October, and spent most of the next week stuck in knee-deep mud.

**The bad weather forced the men of the 7th Panzer to make increasing use of Russian buildings. Diesel fuel, temporarily useless for its primary purpose, was "borrowed" to kill the omnipresent lice. At least one *Landser* even longed for the German flea, so harmless compared to his Russian counterpart (von Manteuffel, 271–72).

*   *   *   *   *

20 October 1941

My dear Mother,

The hour is approaching midnight and I'm writing to you in the dim light of a kerosene lamp. I'm on guard duty tonight. At least then you have the advantage of being alone with your thoughts and can enjoy a comparatively peaceful and quiet time. My thoughts at this late hour are with you at home.

A couple of days ago we were almost totally snowed in and now it has been raining incessantly for twenty-four hours. You should have the opportunity just once to look at this country. Most likely you would only be able to shake your head, no matter if you were looking at the people or at the landscape. When we had the first real cold spell, the people were still walking around barefooted. Most of them have no shoes, but only rags that they wrap around their feet. They do this no matter if it's dry or wet and now in this muddy weather, they're walking around with incredibly dirty rags around their feet. Hygiene is something totally foreign to these people. You folks back home in our beautiful Fatherland cannot imagine what it's like. These people here live together with the animals, indeed they live like animals. If they could only once see a German living room. That would be paradise for them, a paradise that these Communist scoundrels, Jews and criminals have denied them. We have seen the true face of Bolshevism, have gotten to know it and experienced it, and will know how to deal with it in the future. Yes, my dear Mother, there is only one Germany in the world and we hope to return to it soon.

Greetings from your son, Karl

* * * * *

26 October 1941

Dearest Mädi, little Horsti,

I'm enjoying the taste of one of those excellent Nestor cigarettes that you sent me. Thank you very much. Yes, it's Sunday again, but don't ask what the weather is like. Rain, rain, nothing but rain! The countryside looks like an endless gray swamp. The roads, at least what's left of them, have become totally impassable. Even walking has become a feat. It is very difficult to stay on your feet—that's how slippery it is.*

As each day passes we're becoming more and more conscious of Christmas. I suppose we will have to celebrate Christmas out here in soldier fashion, because we no longer believe that we will be able to spend this festival of peace with our loved ones at home. But look, dear Mädi, we really have no reason to complain when we think of our comrades who are at the front stuck in mud, water, and terrible conditions and, nevertheless, ready to beat back the last possible attack of the Russians. They are even ready to pursue them with a quick counterattack.

A great friendship binds us German soldiers together out here. It is this comradery and the support that we're able to give each other that is, in my opinion, the secret behind our incredible successes and victories. This loyalty and devotion to the cause again and again was the decisive factor in many a battle and I tell you, this comradeship has been one of the most magnificent experiences out here. This loyalty is the essence of the German fighting spirit. We can depend on each other unconditionally. Each one of us sets an example for the other and that makes us strong. I've always known of this loyalty, but today it burns in me like a holy flame. Let this loyalty which I've experienced out here in comradeship be the foundation of our future life.**

The rain continues to fall and in spite of the bad weather and the battles, I dream of you. Sometimes I can imagine how at home, during a storm like this, we would all sit together in a cozy corner of our home and how my son would sit on my lap, attempting to pull my hair. You would be sitting next to me, resting your head against my shoulder, and would look at me and the three of us would indeed be extremely happy. Then, when our boy has been put to bed, the rest of the evening would belong to us. I often think of those hours and days at the university in Würzburg where we first met. I think of those strolls we took in the forest after we were engaged. I know that upon my return we will spend many beautiful hours like that again. Mädi, you are my one and only love and my heart belongs to you always. I kiss and hug you.

Your Korri

P.S. Dear Mädi, I have a request for a few things. Perhaps it is my shopping list for Christmas. 1, I need something to read. No works of literature, mind you, just junk, just anything. Something to pass the time. 2, Send some crossword puzzles. 3, I need some candles since there is no electricity out here. All I can give you in return is my love.

*This combination of frost and rain persisted until the end of October in the 7th Panzer Division's sector. It required two weeks to make a single routine move at an average speed of three or four kilometers per hour, and with significant losses of vehicles and other material.

**This attitude, while found among veterans of all armies and all wars, was particularly strong in the *Wehrmacht,* and contributed significantly to the highly praised fighting power and endurance of German troops on all fronts of World War II. At its heart was the deliberate fostering of small-group loyalties, combined with systematic efforts to generate a sense of membership in a *Wehrgemeinschaft* as well as a *Volksgemeinschaft.* Since well before 1914, Germany's military leaders had sought to enhance the identity of army with society, a goal they shared with

National Socialism. (See particularly Manfred Messerschmitt, "The Wehrmacht and the Volksgemeinschaft," *Journal of Contemporary History* 18 (1983), 719–40; and van Creveld, *Fighting Power*.)

* * * * *

1 November 1941
Report on the Defensive Battle of Vyazma*

Written by Sergeant Karl Fuchs

The encircling movement of our troops around the area of Vyazma had been completed. Our fall offensive, conducted with lightning speed, surprised the Russians so much that the enemy found no time to break out of the encirclement. Our tank company had been assigned to support a motorized battalion which occupied the ridges to the west of Vyazma. This battalion held the ridges with great tenacity. On 11 October 1941, an early dawn alarm robbed us of our sleep. Once again the Russians were attempting to break out of the encirclement by attacking the infantry battalion. Within minutes our tanks were on the move and pushed across meadows and fields and through the underbrush toward the danger area. Enemy tanks were sighted. The Second Platoon [Karl's unit] was given the job of reconnoitering. The ridges occupied by our infantry men were under heavy artillery and machine-gun fire. We were in radio contact with the infantry unit and slowly and carefully, like hunters stalking their prey, we moved toward the ridge. A thick ground fog limited our visibility considerably. Suddenly out of the fog to the right of us a huge Russian tank appeared. Damn the fog! We had hardly sighted this monster before it disappeared again like a ghost into the white curtain of fog. At least we knew the direction in which it was moving. Carefully we pursued the monster. Suddenly a gust of wind ripped apart the fog and there it was. Immediately we opened fire, attacking it from several different directions. Clearly we could see our hits, but the monster seemed unharmed. We radioed to headquarters: Engaged in battle with heavy Russian tanks! Two of the Russian tanks turned away from our fire and disappeared into a little valley. The last one became the target of our concentrated fire. Again and again we hit its steel armor until it too turned and fled. The sun then broke through the fog and the valley was in clear view before us. From our advantageous position on the slope we continued attacking the enemy tanks until these monsters were either burning or were left abandoned by their crew. Seven tanks were destroyed or had been inactivated. We changed our position frequently in order to be a different target for the enemy's artillery fire. It also deceived the enemy about our relative strength. If they had known that there were only four of us which prevented the escape of seven of them! Our cannons silenced them. The rest of the company arrived. Our collective fire power destroyed the last elements of enemy resistance. A truck convoy stood ablaze. The crews from eight heavy pieces of artillery, as well as an uncounted number of infantrymen, ran for their lives. Our infantrymen greeted us with open arms. The entire company gathered together and were ready for new orders.

(Signed) Fuchs

*This, the most detailed account of his actual experiences in battle Karl had ever given, reflected desperate and in part successful Russian efforts to break the German barrier and escape eastward. *Panzergruppe 3*, facing increasing difficulties in keeping its forward formations supplied, was unable to cut the lines of retreat completely. On 12 October, the Russians infiltrated the 7th Panzer Division's sector so skillfully that they were once again well into the artillery positions before they were discovered. Desperate hand-to-hand fighting ensued until the 25th Panzer Regiment intervened to restore the line (von Manteuffel, 196ff.).

* * * * *

4 November 1941

Dear Father,

Your letter which arrived today must have been on a real odyssey since it took the letter six weeks to get here. But at least I have news of you. My assumption that you were in the battle area around Kiev was true after all. I guess you have searched in vain for me as well but it seems as if the two of us are competing for bigger and bigger achievements. Our last battle of encirclement against the enemy up here and your experiences in Kiev will never be forgotten. We have never before struck the enemy with such crushing defeats. I guess the Russians never dreamed that we would engage in this kind of an offensive prior to winter. I'm convinced that the last cohesive forces of the enemy have been decimated and once again our Führer has proven to the world that the German soldier can do incredible tasks.

In the quiet evening hours we often think of those comrades who have given their lives for our sacred German cause. You're right, Father, we will never forget them—especially not my best friend, Lieutenant Preussner, with whom I had shared so much joy and sorrow for over two years. The cool earth covers him now but he lives on in me just as your friend Eckstein lives on in you. I'm struck by the similarities and repetitions that take place in our respective lives.

I assume that you will be home much sooner than I. Please greet my son for me and make sure that everything is all right. In the meantime, we stand guard. Let me shake your hand and Sieg Heil!

Your loyal son, Karl

*   *   *   *   *

4 November 1941

My dearest wife, my little Horsti,

Once again it is evening and I'm writing to you in the dim light of my kerosene lamp. I am the only one awake at the moment and no sound but the deep and regular breathing of my comrades can be heard. It's precisely the right atmosphere for me to write.

In front of me on the table is a little clock which shows the time and will remind me when to post the change of guard. This clock continues ticking and is unconcerned about what goes on in the world. One minute after another goes by; then hours, weeks, months, and even years pass and we human beings can do no more than wait for tomorrow, for the future. Sometimes I wish I could turn the clock ahead to that day when I will be allowed to hold you in my arms—never to leave you again. But I suppose in the end, it's a good thing that we human beings can't play with time. Impatient individuals would then move time so far ahead until there wouldn't be any time left and then what? Turn the clock backwards again? I'm glad that nature has its laws and that we can't tinker with them.

If you have an opportunity to buy woolen things for me, please go ahead and do it. I will be very happy to receive them.

In your letter of 13 October, you wrote again about our young son. I can't imagine that he is so big and strong already that he can sit by himself in the corner of the couch! Dear Mädi, what great fortune it is to have such a child. Just wait until I'm home! I will be able to rock him in my arms and won't give him back to you at all! Do you think he'll be astonished to see me in my black tank uniform?

I have to go outside now and make my rounds to make sure that everything is in order. Everytime I'm outside at night I look to the West, hoping that I can see you in the distance. Then I kiss and hug you and long for you.

Your Korri

*   *   *   *   *

5 November 1941
My dear Mädi,

Thanks a lot for that "lovely" letter which I received today. Let me say at the very start I'm by no means annoyed with the letter and the only reason that I'm not madder than hell is because I *won't* be mad. The person who wrote these words is a stranger to me. I simply can't believe that it was you who wrote this letter. At first I wanted to send the letter back but I decided against it because I do want to reply to a number of things that you said. Please take out the letter which you wrote sometime ago and compare it with my answers. You will see that you have misinterpreted me completely. At that time I simply said that if you didn't want to teach school anymore then you should go ahead and quit and simply spend your time taking care of our child.* I've never doubted that you love the profession which you chose. Yet I'm not aware that I ever attempted to instruct you in the art of school teaching. That's why your words are totally incomprehensible to me. I will henceforth refrain from using exaggerated rhetoric, as you say, when I write to the people back home. I suppose we can prove our idealism here in this "magnificent" country and in daily battle. In the future I will spare you the experiences of a soldier at the front. Lastly, let me say that what I intend to teach my pupils in the future is none of your damn business. Apparently you're upset about something that I don't know about; otherwise you wouldn't write this way. Let's assume that you indeed will stop teaching. If you think that you can spend the few lousy Reichsmark that I make every month, then all I can say is: Go right ahead! No, Mädi, you can't threaten me this way. Don't believe that you've married some kind of a clown. If you think that you're stubborn, believe me, I'm more stubborn than you are. How in the world can you say that I belittle your needs and worries and consider them insignificant? If you've ever been unjust to me, this was the time. You write that your love for me has not diminished. I don't get it. It doesn't make any sense. I'm faced with enough nonsense out here every day that I'd just as soon not receive any from home. Don't worry, in the future I won't bother you anymore with personal requests for money, cigarettes and letters.

The best part of your letter, though, is the end. It is reassuring to know that I have a person at home whom I'm totally devoted to and who can assert with a sarcastic smile, I imagine, that spending the winter in Russia must be marvelous and that my son can grow up very well without my help. These words really hurt! Apparently you've grown indifferent to me. I suppose the main thing is, though, that you're leading a dazzling life and are becoming more beautiful from day-to-day. Well, so much for my answers to your letter.

You've promised me in the past that we wouldn't quarrel. The letter today, however, contradicts that promise. I'm willing to forget the entire matter and you must agree when you read your letter again that I won't stand for this kind of language and couldn't take this attack lying down. Mädi, why make life more difficult than it already is? I look forward to every one of your letters and am happier than a kid at Christmas when they come. You must know how much they mean to me. Please don't do this to me again. Do you want to make up? I love you so much, only you.

Your Korri

*See letter of 22 September.

*   *   *   *   *

6 November 1941

Dear Mother,

I was so happy to receive your letter and the two pictures that were included. I've received three other photos from Mädi, one only with Horsti in it, one with you holding my son and the others are pictures of Mädi and Horsti. I have to look at these pictures again and again and then must suppress my longing into the furthest corner of my heart. My son is almost a half-year old! I suppose by the time I see him for the first time he'll be able to walk already.

We've received orders to move on in a few days and again the direction is further away from home.* I guess this means that our dream of coming home at Christmas is over. Therefore you at home must pull together even more and be brave.

An icy wind is howling around our camp. Yes, soon snow and cold will be our constant companions. That's all for today. I send you many greetings.

Your Karl

*The 7th Panzer Division began moving forward again on 9 November, taking advantage of weather cold enough to firm up the roads in its sector of advance. On 16 November, it attacked across the Lama River as part of *Panzergruppe 3*'s last drive on Moscow. Most of the division's combat units were by now at full strength, but their vehicles and weapons alike were so badly worn that final breakdowns were imminent—another indication of the come-as-you-are war Germany was waging in Russia.

*   *   *   *   *

6 November 1941

Dear Father,

Yes, we're moving out again. In spite of terrible cold and snow, our unit has been called up again. At least we know now for sure that we won't be spending Christmas at home. Somewhere in the north here we will find a little Christmas tree and will celebrate Christmas with comrades. We know what our duty is and will be up to the task.

Don't bother looking for me. Suffice it to say that we're

moving in the direction of Moscow. I suppose that you may even be home by now. If you are home, I know that you will set things right.

Mädi and Mother sent me a few pictures of my son. Damn it all, I'd really like to see him soon, but I suppose that I'm in the same situation now that you were in during the Great War. We have to suppress our longing for our loved ones because we're fighting for a great cause. I enjoyed hearing about your adventures. Yes, we too are familiar with partisans and have dealt with them.*

On to new deeds and victories! Sieg Heil.

Your loyal son, Karl

*By this time a combination of Soviet organization, German atrocities, and failure to round up stragglers from the Vyazma-Bryansk pocket had continued to generate vigorous, small-scale partisan activity in the rear of *Panzergruppe 3*. The dense forests in this region facilitated the operation of guerrilla bands, as did the inadequate German security forces. As yet, however, the partisans were by no means the comprehensive threat they became after 1942.

* * * * *

11 November 1941

My dearest, my little boy,

Today is a very happy day for me. It's almost as if I'm back in my childhood because I remember St. Nicholas Day and all the activities associated with it. Starting with St. Nicholas Day, the anticipation of Christmas grows real. I suppose St. Nick thought of me a distant soldier today since I received so many presents. Dear Mädi, I really want to thank you for all the lovely gifts. Let me tell you what they are so that you know that I received them; first of all, many thanks for the cigarettes and please thank Hedi for the few words that she added in your letter. Thank you also for the candy, the toothpaste and the lotion, the woolen gloves and the woolen scarf. I can really use the last two items now.

Yes, here I am again, sitting in one of these God-forsaken, Russian peasant houses supporting my head with my hand and thinking of you, my dear boy and of all those loved ones back home who've been so good to me. And today, our boy is five months old. I suppose that's a birthday of sorts. I can imagine that he has grown big and strong and is a very sweet baby.

All of us out here, all my comrades, continuously ask the all important question—when, when are we going to be able to go home? I still can't give you a definitive answer to that question. When I do return from these battles, I will probably come empty-handed, but my heart will be full of endless love for you and that is probably worth more than any present.

A few days ago it really started to get cold around here. It's a gripping cold and not comparable to anything that we might experience at home.* Yes, we really have to bite the bullet now but we will survive this as well.

I love you forever—you alone and Horsti.

Your Korri

P.S. We will discuss the baptism of our son when I return home. By the way, Horst Bernhard wrote to me that our former residence advisors in Würzburg, Adam Hoos and Georg Un-kelhäuser were killed in battle. I think of them a lot these days.

*Temperatures in *Panzergruppe 3*'s area of operation were reaching minus twenty-five degrees centigrade at night by mid-November.

*   *   *   *   *

12 November 1941

My dear Mother,

Yesterday my son was five months old. You don't know how often I think of him. Soon he will babble his first word, "Mama," and maybe he'll say "Papa" as well, and I, his father, am farther away from home than ever. My plight today is similar to Father's in the Great War. We men out here on the front know what our duty is and act accordingly. All of us have become serious and mature in this struggle for the future of our people. If we won't see our homeland by the end of this year and maybe not right away next year either, then we simply have to endure the disappointment because we know that this sacrifice must be made.

Our thoughts, wishes and dreams fly to you at home and when we men gather out here around a small Christmas tree in a few weeks, our eyes will be bright because we'll know that our homeland and our loved ones can celebrate this feast in peace.

You at home must always keep in mind what would have happened if these hordes had overrun our Fatherland. The horror of this is unthinkable!

We know no fear. The cold is going to be a factor, but we shall endure that too. One of these days we will meet again and no one is looking forward to this more than I.

I send my greetings and remain forever

your loyal son, Karl

*   *   *   *   *

Death Notices

2 December 1941

My dear Mrs. Fuchs,

As leader of the unit to which your husband, Sergeant Karl Fuchs, was assigned, I have the sad duty to inform you that your husband was killed on the field of battle on 21 November 1941.

His heroic death occurred when he was fighting bravely for Greater Germany in the front lines during a heavy battle with Russian tanks. The entire company and I would like to extend our deepest sympathies to you for the terrible loss which has befallen you.

We commiserate and are saddened that fate did not allow Karl to see his little daughter* of whom he was so proud. Be assured, however, that we will never forget your husband who was one of our best and bravest tank commanders and who always fought in an exemplary fashion against the enemy.

We have prepared a dignified resting place for him near the city of Klin, north of Moscow. I hope it will be a small consolation for you when I tell you that your husband gave his life so that our Fatherland may live.** I greet you with sincere compassion.

Lieutenant Reinhardt,
Company Commander

*The child was a son.

**Heinrich Böll, the well-known post-World War II German author, was, like Karl Fuchs, born in 1917. In an article appearing in the West German weekly *Die Zeit,* 6 December 1966, he addresses the "class of 1917." He points out that a male born in that year had but one chance in three to reach his twenty-eighth birthday in 1945.

* * * * *

2 December 1941

Dear Mrs. Fuchs,

In the name of the company, I wish to extend to you our deepest sympathy for the painful loss which has befallen you. Our comrade, Sergeant Karl Fuchs, was killed in the evening of 21 November 1941, during a skirmish with Russian tanks.*

He was one of our best comrades and was popular with his superiors as well as with those whom he commanded. He lives on as a shining example of bravery for the entire company.

His last resting place, as well as the grave of his ammunition loader, were prepared by us in the village of Syrapkoje, in the county of Klin. We also photographed the grave of the hero. As soon as I make copies, I will send you a picture.

I requested that the Non-Commissioned Officers' Association become the godparents of your small daughter.** As soon as the company has more time, I will come back to this subject. We are still engaged in heavy battle with the Russians.

I greet you with sincere compassion.

Förster, Master Sergeant

*The 25th Panzer Regiment led the 7th Panzer Division's drive to encircle Moscow from the north. On 20 November, it cut the Moscow-Kalinin high road, then pushed forward against steadily increasing Russian resistance. Here the regiment made its first acquaintance with the T–34, and discovered the futility of trying to penetrate its armor with the 37–mm and short 75–mm guns that were the best weapons they had. By this time the tanks had outrun the rest of the division and suffered heavy losses in ambushes and small-scale encounters. It was in one of these skirmishes that Karl's tank was knocked out and he was killed.

**An understandable error, considering the number of fatalities.

* * * * *

18 June 1943

To Widow Helene Fuchs, schoolteacher

Included is the silver Tank Assault Medal which your husband, Sergeant Karl Fuchs, earned. We are proud to send this decoration to you as the widow of a former member of our unit.

Signed, Major ———

The young lovers. Karl and Mädi in their wartime best, Spring, 1940.

Rosstal in the Nazi years. This photo, taken in 1940 from the church tower, shows the layout and architecture typical of Franconia's small "home towns" before World War II. Rosstal was undamaged physically, but postwar construction and renovation have altered the town's appearance.

In World War I, Karl's father, Hans Fuchs, flew airplanes like the one on this souvenir postcard. Such mementos, common in Weimar Germany, encouraged nationalism and patriotism.

Hitler especially courted the young. This photo, showing him with a group of Hitler Youth, is part of a series of cigarette cards German children and adolescents collected and traded in much the same fashion as their U.S. counterparts did bubblegum cards.

From the same series as the photo of the Hitler Youth, this features members of the League of German Girls, the female counterpart of the Hitler Youth. The Nazis stressed separation of the sexes and biological determination of gender roles.

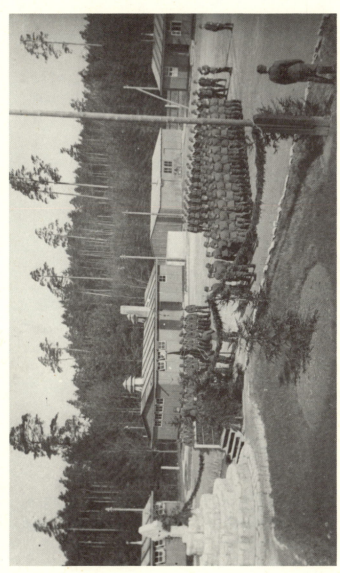

Labor Service recruits are sworn in, 1937. This ceremony was borrowed from the military's oath of allegiance, and highlights the paramilitary character of the program.

Labor Service detachment on its way to work, 1937. Bicycles were used to save time when job sites were far from the camp.

Recruit barracks in Bamberg—typical of the new buildings constructed for Hitler's expanding Wehrmacht.

AT NÜRNBERG, NINE LABOR SERVICE REGIMENTS CARRY THEIR SPADES PAST HITLER STANDING IN HIS MERCEDES-BENZ

This *Life* magazine photo, with spades substituted for rifles in the march past, again shows the military aspects of the Labor Service.

Karl's recruit platoon, Bamberg, 1939.

Wedding photo: Rosstal, market square, April 1940.

German troops in occupied France were enthusiastic tourists. Karl's reservations about French manners and French morals did not deter him from photographing such familiar sights of Paris as Notre Dame.

Karl and Mädi with Karl's father and Mädi's mother, 1941. This was taken in Nuremberg on one of Karl's brief furloughs before his division was sent to Russia.

Karl and two of his crewmen pose before their 38t tank "somewhere in the Rhineland," Spring 1941.

Karl's knocked-out tank. The 38t, like all Wehrmacht tanks in 1941, was extremely vulnerable to Russian antitank guns and depended for safety on its mobility and the skill of its crew.

Snapshot of Karl's grave. The birch cross was virtually a universal symbol of Wehrmacht burials in north and central Russia. Wherever possible, isolated graves such as these were collected in larger military cemeteries.

Sketch of Karl's grave, done in pencil and colored pencil by one of his comrades and sent to the family both as a memento and a possible aid in locating the site. On its back the artist noted: "South of Spass-Saulok (26 kilometers west of Klin)."

6.
Conclusion
by Dennis E. Showalter

Neither British nor American culture has developed a concrete image of the German frontline soldier. His predecessor of the period from 1914 to 1918 is inseparably identified with the characters created by Erich Maria Remarque. For good or ill, Paul Bäumer, Stanislaus Katczinski, Alfred Kropp, Haie Westhus and their comrades, are the stereotypes most readily called to mind when English speakers consider the human aspects of Germany's role in World War I. The later conflict has produced no such dominant work. Hans Hellmut Kirst's anti-heroic Gunner Asch has climbed onto occasional bestseller lists without significantly penetrating the public consciousness anywhere west of the Rhine. Theodore Plivier, Lother Buchheim, and a host of other German novelists present characters so dominated by events that they are submerged in them, failing to stand out in the memory of even dedicated readers of historical fiction. A mixture of pseudo-socialist "realism"—West Germany's equivalent of Britain's angry-young-man school—and a conscious desire on the part of the literate to avoid glorifying any aspect of the Nazi experience combines to discourage the creation of any memorable military portraits in the gallery created by World War II. The German Democratic Republic has been even less hospitable to any fictional treatments of the war that cannot be snugly fitted into party orthodoxy while avoiding offense to the sensibilities of Russian critics, both literary and political.

Shortcomings of written depictions of the frontline experience means the German *Landser* exists visually rather than mentally. He is the blond god riding his tank past disheveled prisoners in 1940, and he is one of an even more bedraggled horde behind allied barbed wire in 1945. He is the sinister SS officer torturing a woman of the resistance, and the helpless man in army gray insisting "We are not all like that" as he looks on. He is the bewildered Sergeant Schultz of *Hogan's Heroes,* the eternally frustrated Afrika Korps lieutenant of *Rat Patrol,* and one of the thoroughgoing professionals who challenge Sergeant Saunders' squad weekly on *Combat.* Above all, he is the opponent, the target, a universal enemy, faceless under his coalscuttle helmet.

Karl Fuchs cannot be called a typical German frontline soldier, because no such person exists outside the constructions of the cliometricians. There are as many individual stories as there were men and women who wore Hitler's uniform. Karl's story can be reconstructed because his family preserved most of his letters. In reading them, it is necessary to remember that they were not intended as a diary or a journal. Karl Fuchs died perceiving all the glory of the Third Reich, aware of none of its bitterness. His was not the kind of critical, probing mind that seeks the fourth side of any three-sided question. Karl was a dreamer who sought beauty in all circumstances. He was an idealist, convinced of the rightness of the cause for which he fought. He was a happy, often an enthusiastic, warrior. He was a beloved son and a freshly minted husband, concerned with keeping his wife and parents reassured of his safety and well-being. Apart from the risks of having his mail censored, this combination of traits made Karl an unlikely source of the horror stories western readers associate with the Russo-German War. Had he survived, his experiences in the east no doubt would have changed him. But whether he would have become more steadfast in his faith or experienced growth through disillusionment remains a subject of speculation. Karl's life can do no more than provide a specific illustration of the general assertion that many Germans who supported the Third Reich did so neither from opportunistic self-interest nor nihilistic delight in destruction, but out of hopes for a better future. For Karl that dream ended in the trampled snow outside of Moscow.

And what remained? Mädi received two letters, hastily written by men concerned with the living rather than the dead. Neither Lieutenant Reinhardt nor *Spiess* Förster were able to remember whether the child of whom Korri was so proud was a boy or girl. The grave they so carefully described was destroyed, either by the *Wehrmacht* in retreat or by a vengeful Soviet government anxious to obliterate even mute traces of German conquest. Hans Fuchs talked of searching for his boy's body, but that was an impossible dream in the winter of 1941–1942. What remained were the letters—and a son who forty years later collected, translated, and edited them, inspired by love for a man he never knew. What remained was a wife who reopened long-healed wounds, sharing her deepest memories in order that Karl Fuchs might be more than a war memory. Her willingness to make possible this contribution to our understanding of the Third Reich indicates a commitment to knowledge and understanding that Karl would have admired.

7.

Glossary of German Terms

Alter Hase	Lit. old hare; experienced, clever soldier
Alter Kämpfer	Lit. old warrior; early party supporter—i.e., the "old guard" of National Socialism
Angestellte	White-collar employee
Arbeitsdienst	Labor service
Beamtentum	Officialdom, civil service
Bierlieder	Drinking songs
Bildung	All-around education
Bildungsroman	A kind of novel in which the all-around education of the main character is the central theme
Bürgermeister	Mayor
Deutschtum	German nationality, cultural identity
Ehebett	Nuptial bed
Fliegerkorps	Lit. air corps; operational unit of the Luftwaffe equivalent to the RAF Group, USAAF Tactical Air Command
Freundschaftsspiel	Friendly match, an exhibition game not counting for standings or championships
Führer	Leader
Gasthaus	Inn, tavern
Gauleiter	National Socialist district leader, area commander
Gleichschaltung	Political and institutional coordination, conversion of dissenters, elimination of opponents
Gottgläubigkeit	Nazi belief in a Christian (warrior) god who stands above denominational differences
Grosstadt	Large city

Glossary of German Terms (cont.)

Gymnasium	Secondary school with classical bias for university aspirants
Jahrgang	Age group, year's class
Kampfzeit	Time of Nazi Party struggle, years before the seizure of power in 1933
Kesselschlacht	Battle of encirclement
Klassenstaat	State made up of disparate and conflicting classes, as opposed to a community in which classes are irrelevant
Kristallnacht	Lit. night of crystal; used to describe the pogrom of 9 November 1938
Landser	A frontline soldier; G.I., Tommy, Grunt
Luftwaffe	Air Force
Machtergreifung	The Nazi seizure of power
Mein Kampf	Lit. my struggle; title of Adolf Hitler's book
Mensur	A duel; proper distance between two duelists
Mittelstand	The middle class
Panzergruppe	Lit. Armored Group; formation that controls two or three armored corps
Pfennig	Penny
Realgymnasium	Secondary school for white-collar aspirants
Reichsdeutsche	Germans living outside of Nazi Germany's borders
Reichsführerschulen	Special party schools for the training of youth elite party cadres
Reichsmark, RM, Mark	Currency in the Third Reich
Reichsparteitag	Nazi Party rally
Reichstag	German Parliament
Reichswehr	German military forces during Weimar Republic
Schwärmer	A romantic dreamer
Schwärmerei	Rapture
Spiess	Sergeant-major (slang)

Glossary of German Terms (cont.)

Stadtkommandant	Commanding officer of an occupied town
Stammtisch	Table reserved for regular customers
SA (Sturmabteilung)	Storm troopers; party militia
Turn- und Sportverein	Athletic club
Volk	People, nation; race
Völkisch	Pure German, anti-Semitic
Volksgemeinschaft	Community of pure Germans
Volksgenosse	Fellow countryman; term of public address
Volksschule	Elementary school
Volkstumspolitik	Politics geared to preserve nationhood and national characteristics
Wehrgemeinschaft	Military community functioning by virtue of its own internal dynamics, as opposed to imposed discipline
Wehrkreis	Military district. Germany was divided into eighteen of them in 1939. Fifteen were geographic; the other three (14, 15 and 16) were nonterritorial and controlled the mobile troops. For most of the war each *Wehrkreis* was responsible for organizing, training, and reinforcing specific divisions
Wehrmacht	The German armed forces
Weimar Republik	Government of Germany from 1919–1933
Werktagsschule	Elementary school with emphasis on practical education

8.

Suggestions for Further Reading

For those interested in pursuing some of the questions raised or suggested in the letters and their commentary, the editors offer the following selection of recent works. As far as possible, the references have been confined to books or articles in English. Choices have also been made with an eye to standards of readability higher than these in the general run of university press publications, and levels of availability beyond university libraries.

Ian Kershaw, *The Nazi Dictatorship Problems and Perspectives of Interpretation* (Baltimore, Md., 1983), is the best current survey of the literature, though the text is hard to follow. Among specific analyses of the nature of National Socialist support, Michael Kater, *The Nazi Party* (Harvard, 1984); and Thomas Childers, *The Nazi Voter: The Social Foundation of Facism in Germany, 1918–1933* (Chapel Hill, N.C., 1983), are the best of the recent interpretations asserting the lower middle-class nature of Nazi support. Richard Hamilton, *Who Voted for Hitler* (Princeton, 1982), effectively challenges that hypothesis by stressing the importance of wider causal variables, including local newspapers' editorial policies. Peter Merkl, *Political Violence Under the Swastika: 581 Early Nazis* (Princeton, 1975), presents the human side of the movement's "Old Fighters" on the basis of the Abel material mentioned above on pages 8 and 9. His book provides a useful context for the life and attitudes of Hans Fuchs. Peter Loewenberg's article, "The Psychological Origins of the Nazi Youth Combat," *American Historical Review* 76 (1971), 1457–1502, neglects sons of party members, boys like Karl, who grew to maturity in the 1920s and early 1930s. Hannsjoachim Koch, *The Hitler Youth: Origins and Development, 1922–1945* (London, 1975) and Peter Stachura, *Nazi Youth in the Weimar Republic* (Santa Barbara, 1975), describe the gradual integration of young men into a totalitarian system. Walter Laqureur, *Young Germany: A History of the German Youth Movement* (London, 1962), remains worthwhile for ideas and attitudes influencing Germany's young men.

Recent research has clearly established the uniqueness of the Nazification process in every region of Germany. As yet, no comprehensive study focusing on the Rosstal region exists. Rainer Hambrecht, *Der Aufstieg der NSDAP in Mittel- und Oberfranken (1925–1933)* (Nürnberg, 1976), is comprehensive for the period before the *Machtergreifung*. For the years after 1933, Ian Kershaw, *Popular Opinion and Political Dissent in the Third Reich* (Oxford, 1983), has a heavy Bavarian accent; and E. N. Peterson, *The Limits of Hitler's Power* (Princeton, 1969), remains useful for its Bavarian case studies.

The complex problem of *Gleichschaltung,* and the related issue of whether Hitler's regime might legitimately be described as revolutionary, were first raised in David Schoenbaum's still excellent *Hitler's Social Revolution (Class and Status) in Nazi Germany 1933–39* (New York, 1966). The best critique of this approach is Jeremy Noake's "Nazism and Revolution," in *Revolutionary Theory and Political Reality,* edited by Noel O'Sullivan (London, 1983), 73–100.

There are fewer good treatments of the Wehrmacht's internal dynamics than might be expected. Martin van Creveld, *Fighting Power* (Westport, Conn., 1982), is a sound introduction despite its exaggerated support for German methods in comparison to U. S. approaches. For the armed forces in which Karl served, Charles Messenger, *The Art of Blitzkrieg* (London, 1976); and Matthew Cooper and James Lucas, *Panzer: The Armoured Force of the Third Reich* (New York, 1976), are among the best of many books on doctrine, organization, and operations.

Karl's images and impressions of occupied France can usefully be evaluated in the context of Richard Cobb's *French and German, German and French: A Personal Interpretation of France Under Two Occupancies, 1914–1918, 1940–1944* (Hanover, N.H., 1983). Better than any other work, this study establishes the human interactions characterizing occupation in both world wars.

For Operation Barbarossa, Albert Seaton, *The Russo-Ger-*

man War (1941–1945) (London, 1971), and John Keegan, *Barbarossa: Invasion of Russia, 1941* (New York, 1970), remain sound introductions. Paul Carell, *Hitler Moves East, 1941–1943*, translated by Ewald Osey (Boston, 1964), is familiar, but tends towards glamorization—a fact reflecting the author's wartime role as press chief of the Nazi Foreign Office. Seaton's *The Battle for Moscow, 1941–1942* (London, 1971) helps put the role of Karl's 7th Panzer Division in an operational context. The ongoing lack of a study of the human aspects of the Russo-German War is only partly met by James Lucas, *War and the Eastern Front. The German Soldier in Russia, 1941–1945* (London, 1979). Omer Bartov, *The Eastern Front, 1941–45: German Troops and the Barbarisation of Warfare* (New York, 1986), emphasizes the impact of ideology at the expense of what veterans call "the filth of war" [*Schmutz des Krieges*].